REAL ESTATE BUYING/SELLING GUIDE
FOR BRITISH COLUMBIA

REAL ESTATE BUYING/SELLING GUIDE
FOR BRITISH COLUMBIA

E. Syberg-Olsen, LL.B.

Self-Counsel Press
(a division of)
International Self-Counsel Press Ltd.
Canada   U.S.A.

Printed in Canada

First edition: April, 1972
Tenth edition: July, 1992
Eleventh edition: June, 1994

Canadian Cataloguing in Publication Data
    Syberg-Olsen, E. 1944 -
        Real estate buying/selling guide for British Columbia

        (Self-counsel legal series)
        ISBN 0-88908-498-X

    1. House buying — British Columbia 2. House selling —
    British Columbia 3. Vendors and purchasers —
    British Columbia — Popular works. I. Title. II. Series.
    HD1379.S92   1994   333.33'09711   C94-910348-9

Self-Counsel Press
(a division of)
International Self-Counsel Press Ltd.
Head and Editorial Office
1481 Charlotte Road
North Vancouver, British Columbia V7J lHl

U.S. Address
1704 N. State Street
Bellingham, Washington 98225

CONTENTS

TABLES

SAMPLES

NOTICE TO READERS

Laws are constantly changing. Every effort is made to keep this publication as current as possible. However, neither the author nor the publisher can accept any responsibility for changes to the law or practice that occur after the printing of this publication. Please be sure that you have the most recent edition.

Note: The fees quoted in this book are correct at the date of publication. However, fees are subject to change without notice. For current fees, please check with the appropriate government office nearest you.

FOREWORD

If you are thinking about either buying or selling your home, or even if you are already a home owner, this book could be invaluable to you not only in terms of providing answers but also in terms of saving money!

No doubt you are already aware that, for most people, the purchase of a home represents the largest single expenditure of their lifetime, and, once purchased, a home represents their main asset. As such, home ownership deserves careful consideration. Yet many people purchase or sell their homes without really understanding what they are doing.

You should ask yourself the following questions: What can a real estate agent do for me? How much can I afford to pay? How can I save money? How much should I accept? What should I look for when selecting a home? What is an interim agreement? How do I find mortgage money? What is the best type of mortgage for me? What government assistance can I get? Do I need a lawyer and, if so, what can a lawyer do for me? What income tax considerations should I be aware of?

The aim of this book is to provide answers to these and many other questions and to provide useful, practical information for the buyer or seller of property. Several areas of law will be discussed, as well as the things that the lawyer or notary does in a real estate transaction. This book, however, is not designed to make anyone a conveyancing expert, but rather to familiarize you with the subject and demonstrate to you the importance of getting professional guidance and assistance when needed.

1
HOUSING — COST AND THE HOME PURCHASER

a. SO YOU WISH TO BUY A HOUSE!

One of the biggest problems many people face today is finding acceptable accommodation in a world of ever-increasing competition for housing and ever-spiralling costs.

Many people wish to own their own accommodation rather than rely on the vagaries of rental accommodation. But before buying a house you should first learn everything you can about the type of housing that is most suitable for your circumstances, the costs involved, how to obtain mortgage monies, the steps to be taken to complete a purchase, and the pitfalls you might encounter. That, in a nutshell, is the aim of this book.

The single most important factor in home ownership is cost. The cost can be divided into two main categories: the initial cost and the continuing costs.

The initial cost is the sales or purchase price together with the acquisition costs, such as legal fees, taxes, and moving expenses. The sales or purchase price is usually determined by the replacement cost of the building and the land (including the costs of providing services like water, sewers, roads, and sidewalks, not to mention other municipal assessments, such as cost development charges). A mark-up is then added to produce the final cost to the purchaser.

The continuing costs are such things as mortgage payments, property taxes, upkeep and maintenance, insurance, etc. These will be discussed in more detail in the next section.

The growth in these costs has forced many people to consider less expensive housing, such as duplexes, condominiums, cooperative housing, townhouses, and mobile homes, as an alternative to the fully detached house. These other forms of housing are primarily an attempt to use available land and construction material more efficiently, so that the total cost of housing can be decreased.

Again, it is the aim of this book to provide current and practical information about various forms of home ownership and the best procedure for achieving such ownership. It is hoped that such information will help you avoid pitfalls and save money when buying a home.

b. HOW MUCH SHOULD YOU SPEND ON HOUSING?

It is generally accepted that a family should spend no more than one-third of its total gross income on the continuing costs of "housing." This figure may vary from individual to individual, depending on other financial commitments but, for the vast majority of people, this figure should not be exceeded. In arriving at the amount that you can afford to spend on housing, you should include the cost of the following items:

(a) Mortgage payments

(b) Property taxes

(c) Fire and liability insurance

(d) Heating, electricity, and water charges

(e) Maintenance — including interior and exterior repainting and occasional repair of the roof and of electrical, plumbing, and heating systems

(f) Gardening

In the case of condominiums (see chapter 7) some of the above (e.g., fire and liability insurance, exterior repair, and gardening) would be included in the monthly strata fee payment.

1. Mortgage payments

Generally the interest rate of the mortgage is set for a determined period or term at the time the mortgage is arranged, so the mortgage payment is usually a fixed expense over the term of the mortgage. In conventional mortgages, part of the mortgage payment is applied against the current accumulated interest, while the remaining part is applied against the principal sum borrowed (the "principal"). When mortgage payments cover only principal and interest, they are referred to as "P.I." payments. The mortgage is dealt with in detail in chapter 5.

2. Property taxes

Many mortgage lenders stipulate in their mortgage that they will pay the property taxes, because they can then ensure that the property taxes are paid. In such cases, and assuming one has a conventional mortgage with monthly payments, one-twelfth of the estimated yearly taxes is added to the total monthly mortgage payments. Such a mortgage is called a "P.I.T." (principal, interest, and taxes) mortgage. The payments on such a mortgage will vary from year to year depending on the rise in property taxes.

When a mortgage company requires taxes to be paid on a monthly basis, the prospective borrower (or mortgagor) should ask how such tax payments will be treated by the mortgage company. Some mortgage companies will apply the total P.I.T. payment toward payment of interest and reduction of the mortgage and then add the amount of the taxes they subsequently pay back onto the then reduced balance.

Others will simply take the tax portion of the P.I.T. payment and put it into a special tax account where it will accumulate until the tax payment is due. Some mortgage companies pay interest on such tax accounts, while others will

3

not. This should, therefore, be taken into account when computing the overall cost of the mortgage.

If the property taxes are not included in the mortgage, you would be wise to set aside a monthly amount which, after one year, would cover the yearly property taxes. Many people who do not do this find themselves unable to suddenly raise the money at tax time and consequently are forced to either borrow the outstanding amount or pay the late payment penalty.

Some municipalities recognize the hardship this can cause and have now instituted a procedure where one can pay property taxes on a monthly basis without incurring any additional cost. This has the additional benefit to the municipality of providing it with a more even flow of revenue.

The cost of taxes for any particular piece of property can be obtained from the municipality in which the property is located. As a very rough general rule, count on approximately 1% of the value of the property annually.

Also, remember when budgeting for this that taxes have historically escalated on a yearly basis by at least 5% to 10%.

3. Fire and liability insurance

The standard home-owner fire insurance policy not only insures against damage by fire to the dwelling, but also against loss on the contents of the house, and it provides comprehensive personal liability. The amount of the insurance carried should cover the replacement value of the building that is to be insured — as opposed to the purchase price of the "house" which would also include the land. The land, of course, does not need to be insured against fire.

The amount of insurance carried under some policies automatically increases every year to take into account the rising replacement cost due to inflation. Although some policies are written for a three-year period, with the premium payable in advance, it is now more common to see policies written for one year only.

When gauging the cost of insurance, you should remember that not only are insurance rates subject to change, but also, as replacement values escalate, an increase in insurance coverage will result in a corresponding increase in the premium. Please note that coverage for stamps, jewellery, and other such items — as well as earthquake damage — is, in most instances, not included unless specifically requested. If included, an additional premium will be incurred.

4. Utility charges

In calculating the approximate amount of utility charges, you should remember to average these out over the entire year, as both heating and electricity (and, in some cases, water charges, where they are metered) will vary according to the season. For estimating purposes, be sure to obtain this information from the vendor before submitting an offer. You may be wise to request receipts, as many property owners' estimates of their charges are only wild guesses. Remember, too, that utility rates are subject to increases.

5. Maintenance

Although it is impossible to determine the exact amount required for maintenance and repairs, it is wise to allocate a monthly figure in excess of the bare maintenance costs. Remember, it is impossible to anticipate all expenses, and some amount should be allowed for "major replacement" expenditures. In arriving at a realistic amount, you should consider how often the interior and exterior will need repainting or refinishing, how often floor coverings such as linoleum or carpet will need replacing, how often plumbing or electrical wiring will need to be repaired, how often the furnace or hot water tank will need an overhaul, etc.

6. Gardening

In estimating gardening expenses, as well as considering the cost of maintaining the garden, do not forget to include the initial cost of garden equipment such as lawn mowers, edgers, rakes, shears, shovels, ladders, and hoses.

7. Don't forget those initial expenses

We have just looked at the continuing expenses of owning a house once it has been acquired. However, there are several initial expenses that should also be considered.

(a) Moving costs

(b) The need for appliances such as a refrigerator, stove, dishwasher, washer, and dryer

(c) Redecorating costs, including carpets and draperies

(d) Legal fees and disbursements

(e) Loan fees or mortgage commitment fees

(f) Other adjustments between vendor and purchaser

(g) Property transfer tax

The above are self-explanatory with the exception of (f) and (g). The property transfer tax is dealt with in its own section below. "Other adjustments" would include additional money that the purchaser is required to pay the vendor. These are usually reimbursements of expenses that the vendor has prepaid on behalf of the purchaser — such as fuel oil in the tank, fire insurance (if the purchaser is assuming the vendor's policy), prepaid taxes, and water rates.

Adjustments of these items are covered between the vendor and the purchaser in a document known as the "Statement of Adjustments." This statement adjusts figures and amounts owed by both parties as of the adjustment date, and it is usually prepared by the purchaser's lawyer. (This document will be discussed in further detail later.) As these items are additional expenses that are not included in the down payment, you, as the purchaser, should be very careful before committing your entire savings to such a down payment. You should pay particular attention to the property transfer tax.

8. Property transfer tax

The property transfer tax is calculated on the fair market value of the property being acquired and is paid by the purchaser at the time application is made to register in the Land Title Office. The tax is imposed at a rate of 1% on the first $200 000 of the fair market value of the property being transferred and 2% of the balance of the fair market value. Accordingly, for a house worth $100 000, the property transfer tax is $1 000, while on a house worth $300 000, the tax is $4 000. It must be emphasized that this tax is payable in full, in cash, right in the beginning when the property is being registered. The tax is payable —

(a) where there is a change in registered owner of a property,

(b) for any leasehold interest in a property where the duration of the lease including any options or extension or renewals exceeds three years (although an exception is provided for leases of more than 30 years),

(c) on registration of agreements for sale,

(d) on cancellations of agreements for sale,

(e) on registration of a life estate interest, and

(f) on Crown grants and Crown leases

There are certain transactions that are exempt. Some of the more common are —

(a) first-time home buyers for homes valued up to $250 000 in the Lower Mainland and $200 000 for the rest of the province (for more information about the First-Time Buyers Program, please call the Ministry of Finance and Corporate Relations in Victoria at (604) 387-1500),

(b) transfers between related individuals of a principal residence, a recreational residence, or family farm,

(c) a transfer of property pursuant to a separation agreement or court order in the Family Relations Act,

(d) a transfer pursuant to the completion of a registered agreement for sale where the tax was paid on the registration of the Agreement for Sale, and

(e) transmission of property to the survivor of a joint tenancy.

Since their inception, the property transfer tax rules have been amended to provide relief in instances where a principal residence is purchased with high ratio financing (i.e., more than 75% financing — see section **d.** of chapter 6).

The amount of the tax relief is 4% of the difference between the financed amount (with an allowable limit of 95% of the fair market value) and 75% of the fair market value of the property. For example, if the property has a fair market value of $100 000, the normal property transfer tax would be $1 000. If this property were financed to 95% or $95 000, the relief is equal to 4% of the difference between $95 000 and $75 000, being 75% of the fair market value. The difference in this example amounts to $20 000, so the relief would be 4% of this amount or $800. The purchasers would therefore be paying a property transfer tax of only $200 calculated as follows:

$1 000 (being normal property transfer tax) less $800 (being amount of relief) = $200

To qualify for this relief, the following must be met:

(a) The value of the principal residence cannot exceed $150 000 or $200 000 if the property is located in the Greater Vancouver Regional District, the Central Fraser Valley Regional District, or the Dewdney-Allouette Regional District.

8

(b) No more than $5 000 of the amount borrowed can be repaid ($6 650 if the property is located within the Lower Mainland Regional Districts) during the year following registration of the purchase.

(c) The purchaser or the purchaser's spouse has resided in British Columbia for at least 12 months prior to registration.

(d) The registered financing exceeds 75% of the fair market value of the property and is registered concurrently with the transfer to purchase the property.

(e) The purchaser intends to occupy the principal residence for at least one year after registration.

(f) The acquisition of the principal residence is accomplished by registration of an estate in fee simple, agreement for sale, or prepaid lease.

(g) The amount borrowed has a term of at least one year from the date of registration.

(h) To obtain the relief, an application must accompany the registration.

9. Goods and services tax (GST)

Nothing is sure but death and more taxes and the 7% federal goods and services tax (GST) does apply to most types of new housing. Because of the complexity of the rules surrounding the GST, the following comments only apply to residential real estate.

The only things the tax department didn't get its claws into were used residential properties, personal-use property such as cottages and hobby farms, and land not purchased from a developer. Sales of new and substantially renovated residential housing including the land component and costs of related services such as legal fees to register title will be subject to GST.

However, the government is currently allowing a partial rebate as an attempt to keep the GST from becoming a barrier to affordable housing. The rebate is 36% of the tax paid on new housing costing $350 000 or less to a maximum rebate of $8 750. For housing costing between $350 000 and $450 000, the maximum rebate is decreased by $87.50 for every $1 000 the purchase price exceeds $350 000. For new housing costing more than $450 000, there is no rebate.

The rebate applies when both the land and the house are purchased from a builder or if GST was paid on both. If, however, GST was not paid on the land but only on the house, the rebate for properties valued under $350 000 will be the lesser of $1 720 or 10% of the GST paid on the house. Again, phase-provisions apply between the same levels as described above. The rebate is obtainable by direct application or by assignment to the builder. Assigning the rebate to the builder will avoid financing the tax.

The exemption for used residential homes would in all likelihood still apply even if the home was also used for commercial purposes such as, for example, running a business from the house, provided the dwelling was "primarily" residential. If more than 50% of the home was used for commercial purposes, only the residential portion would be exempt and the balance would be taxable.

To complicate things further, for used residential housing or personal-use real estate, it is the vendor's use of the property that determines whether the sale is exempt. Although most purchasers will expect used residential property or personal-use property to be exempt, the purchasers will be liable for the GST if any is due. To avoid this potential uncertainty and liability, the vendor should be required to provide to the purchasers a statement or certificate which confirms the GST situation of the property. If a false statement is provided, the vendor will be liable for the tax. The purchasers will thus be relieved of the liability provided they have exercised due care and diligence in accepting the validity of the vendor's statement. This statement can be put in the interim agreement if it is not already contained in the pre-printed form.

Remember, GST liability can be a confusing area and the cost of mistakes is high, so if you are at all unsure, seek professional assistance.

10. Adding it all up

Let's use an example to illustrate how a prospective purchaser can determine an affordable price range for a home. Harry and Hilda Homeseeker have saved $26 000 and now wish to purchase a house. Harry and Hilda both work and make approximately $46 000 in combined gross income per year. Harry expects that he will be making that by himself in approximately two years when they expect Hilda to stop working and have a family.

They think they will have to purchase appliances for about $2 500 and have estimated that their other initial expenses, including property transfer tax of $1 000 and legal fees of $800, will be about $3 500 — a total outlay of $6 000. This will leave them with a down payment of $26 000 - $6 000 = $20 000, or less if GST was payable on their home.

Thirty percent of their gross income is $13 800 per year or $1 150 per month. Harry and Hilda should, therefore, be able to spend approximately $1 150 per month on housing without overextending themselves.

The Homeseekers have calculated that, for a house in their price range, their net property taxes would be $1 200 per year or $100 per month.

This reduces the amount available monthly for mortgage payments from $1 150 to $1 050. A conventional mortgage amortized (calculated according to the length of time that it takes to repay the mortgage based on fixed payments and at a fixed interest rate) over 25 years at 12% interest requires monthly payments of approximately $1 050 for every $101 700 borrowed (see Table #1 in chapter 6).

$$\frac{\$1\ 050 \times 1\ 000}{10.32} = \$101\ 744$$

However, if interest on the mortgage is 6%, approximately $156 716 can be obtained with monthly payments of $1 050:

$$\frac{\$1\ 050 \times 1\ 000}{6.70} = \$156\ 716$$

Therefore, Harry and Hilda Homeseeker should not spend more on a house than $101 700 plus $20 000 or $121 700 if the interest rate on their mortgage is 12%, but could spend $176 700 ($156 700 plus $20 000) if they are able to obtain mortgage funds at 6½%. (See also Tables #1 and #2 in chapter 6.)

This example and the generally accepted rules apply to the average family situation. It goes without saying that if a person is already heavily in debt, these ratios will not work. Likewise, they will not work without a sacrifice of some sort if an extraordinary amount of income is usually spent on hobbies or other items.

Most prospective home buyers fall in love with, and want to buy, the home that is just a little bit above their budget. This overreaching will, in many cases, not be discouraged by the real estate agent whose commission is based on the sale price.

Some people will unwisely argue that such overreaching is justified, as inflation will undoubtedly mean salary increases. Therefore, they rationalize that as time goes by they will be better able to afford the house. Unfortunately, it is not always possible to foresee financial setbacks or a sudden and drastic increase in the mortgage rate and monthly payments, which, in the case of the overextended purchaser, could result in a severe crunch and possibly in a foreclosure action.

After considering all this and deciding on the price range for your "dream home," you should now locate and purchase it. To better understand what you are getting into, however, it is essential for you to know some basic facts about contract law.

2

CONTRACTS AND REAL ESTATE

a. HOW IMPORTANT ARE CONTRACTS?

The reason for dealing with contracts at this stage is that once the decision has been made to purchase a house and the price range has been determined, the purchase will be initiated by means of an "offer to purchase," which becomes the "interim agreement" after acceptance by the seller.

This document is probably the most important legal document you will ever sign. It is a contract — a fully enforceable and legally binding contract! Once signed and accepted, it will govern the entire transaction and determine the obligations and rights of the parties involved until the transaction is completed and, in most instances, even afterwards.

For this reason, the interim agreement should be considered not only as the first step of the transaction, but also as the support of the whole staircase. Just as the staircase will topple if the support gives way, so the transaction will crumble if the interim agreement is faulty.

Contracts are not just the monopoly of "Philadelphia lawyers" to be read and executed behind impenetrable walls in somber, oak-panelled boardrooms. Every commercial transaction — from buying an ice cream cone to purchasing an apartment building, to engaging a plumber, to signing a star hockey player — is governed by contract law and includes all the elements of a contract.

b. THE ELEMENTS OF CONTRACTS

In order to create a valid contract, *all* of the following elements must be present:

(a) Mutual agreement

(b) Consideration or seal

(c) Legal capacity in the parties

(d) Lawful object

(e) Intention of the parties to create legal and enforceable obligations

In fact, it may surprise you to learn that these elements are present in every transaction. Take, for instance, the case of Gus Zeller who wants to purchase a case of beer. He picks out the beer and takes it to the cashier who rings up the price on the cash register. Gus pays the cashier and leaves with his beer.

Whether or not you realize it, the following things took place: Gus wanted to purchase a case of beer; the liquor store, represented by the cashier, wanted to sell a case of beer; the price, delivery date, and time was agreed upon so that there was, therefore, mutual agreement. Gus's consideration was the payment of the price to the liquor store; the consideration of the liquor store was the transfer of the ownership of the beer to Gus and, as Gus was over 19 years of age, both Gus and the liquor store had legal capacity to enter into the transaction. Since there is nothing illegal about purchasing beer from a liquor store, the object of the contract was lawful. It was, furthermore, Gus's intention to keep the beer and the liquor store's intention to keep the money and, as both parties intended to be bound by their arrangement, point (e) was satisfied.

Let us explore these items in further detail.

1. Mutual agreement

Before there can be mutual agreement, there must first be an offer, which must be accepted. Both the offer and the acceptance must be made with an intention to be bound. The offer must also be specific as to the terms and the conditions. The offer and the acceptance can be made either orally or in writing or even by the mere conduct of the parties (subject to the B.C. Statute of Frauds, which is discussed later).

The best way to illustrate the above is through examples. Picture for a moment our friends Harry and Gus meeting on the street as Gus is on his way home from the liquor store. The following exchange takes place:

"Hi, Harry, old boy. How are things?"

"Pretty good, Gus. And yourself?...I see you're still in high spirits."

"Say, Harry, it's a good thing I ran into you. I wanted to ask you about your car. I understand that you want to sell it...and I would like to buy it."

"Yes, I would like to sell it."

(At this stage there is still no mutual agreement, as neither party has agreed on any of the details of the transaction, such as which of Harry's cars they are talking about, the price of the car, how it is to be paid for, or the delivery date.)

"How much are you asking for that blue Ford of yours?"

"$2 000 cash on delivery."

(If, at this stage, Gus accepted, paid Harry a deposit, and told Harry that he would be around in the morning with the remainder to pick up the car, a contract would have been created.) Suppose, however, that the conversation continued as follows:

"I like your car, but I only have $1 800 and I'm prepared to pay you that in cash."

(At this point an offer has almost been made and various things could develop depending on how Gus finishes off his sentence.) Suppose Gus continued,

"...and I will pay you the money tomorrow at 3:00 p.m. provided you let me know if my offer is acceptable by 12:00 p.m. today."

(Unless Harry accepts the offer within the time limit specified, the offer would lapse at the specified time and be null and void. That is, the offer would not be binding on Gus if Harry accepted it at 1:00 p.m. instead of 12:00 p.m.) Suppose, however, Gus had continued and said,

"...Think about it and, if you decide yes, let me know and I will bring the money over and pick up the car."

(The offer would lapse unless it was accepted within a reasonable length of time. That is, Harry couldn't wait a year until his car had depreciated to $1 500 and then phone Gus and accept his offer of $1 800.)

The offer would, of course, also lapse if either Harry (the "offeree") or Gus (the "offeror") died, or if Harry plainly refused the offer.

If Harry had counter-offered by saying to Gus, "$1 900 and you've got a deal!" he would immediately have terminated the original offer and would then not have been able to accept the original offer unless it was made again. However, instead of counter-offering, Harry might have said:

"If I invite you home for a cup of coffee, do you think I could talk you into $1 900?"

In that case, the original offer would not, in all likelihood, be terminated, as this is really a request for information, and a request for information does not terminate an offer.

It must be remembered that the acceptance, to make an offer into a binding contract, must be unqualified. Thus, if Harry had said, "I accept your offer of $1 800 provided you

17

also buy my snow tires and rims for $100," Harry's reply would have been a counter-offer and would not be binding upon Gus unless he chose to accept it.

Once an offer is made it can be revoked by the offeror any time prior to acceptance of the offer by the offeree *provided* notice is given of such revocation to the offeree. Thus, in the situation where Harry was given until 12:00 p.m. the following day to accept the offer, Gus would have been able to phone Harry at 10:00 a.m. and tell him that he had decided to revoke his offer. If, however, Harry managed to tell Gus that he had decided to accept his offer before Gus could revoke it, Gus would technically be bound to complete the transaction, as once acceptance has been made it is too late to revoke the offer.

Before leaving the subject of offers, mention should also be made of advertisements. An advertisement is not considered as an offer but as an *invitation* to make an offer. Therefore, if an advertisement appeared in the paper advertising new cars for $20, a person would not be able to enforce a sale or insist on delivery at that price. However, if the advertisement was purposely misleading, the dealership might be guilty of fraudulent advertising...but that is a completely different matter.

Remember that acceptance must be communicated unless the offer provides otherwise. Thus, if Gus had said to Harry, "Unless I hear from you by 12:00 p.m. tomorrow, I will consider the offer accepted," there would have been no acceptance of the offer unless Harry specifically had agreed to that form of arrangement.

Not only must acceptance be communicated, it must also be communicated in the way asked for by the offeror. Therefore, as long as an offer is accepted in the way called for in the offer, the offeror is bound even if he or she does not actually physically receive the acceptance. For example, if the offer calls for acceptance by mail and the offeror does so, the contract is accepted once the letter is posted, even if the offeror never receives the acceptance. This is so since the offeror has specified the use of the mail and by doing so, is deemed to take the risk of non-delivery. This, of course, would be subject to the offeror's being able to prove the acceptance was actually posted. (This should not be confused with a revocation which must actually reach the offeree before he or she accepted.)

Although the discussion has concerned itself primarily with the sale of Harry's car to Gus, all the principles discussed apply equally to a real estate contract. Thus, if an offer in an interim agreement specifies that an acceptance of the offer can be made by leaving a signed copy of the interim agreement at your place of residence, you, the offeror, are bound by that action, regardless of whether or not you actually get the signed copy. The offeree just has to be able to prove that he or she left it there!

To sum up, the essence of a contract or an agreement is that the parties must agree to the same thing. The offer and acceptance, therefore, must clearly specify all the details of the agreement.

2. Consideration or seal

In law, a promise (contract or agreement) is binding only if the promise is made either "under seal" or in return for a benefit of some sort to the person making the promise. This benefit is commonly called "consideration."

Formerly, a seal attached to the document was usually an impressive-looking red wax mass in which an impression had been made by a seal while the wax was still hot. The seal commonly used today is an unimposing red sticker glued to the document beside the signature line. The seal signifies the intention of the parties to create legal relations between them.

Consideration can be described as something the person making the promise receives in return for such a promise. The "something" can be another promise in return, an act, or any other thing of value to the promissor. Certain basic rules have evolved in English contract law (from where we derive most of our legal principles), and one of these states that if a person provides no consideration to a contract, that person cannot take part in that contract.

Illustration

Suppose Tom, Dick, and Harry are all parties to an agreement in which Harry promises Tom and Dick that he will pay Tom $100 if Dick will paint Harry's kitchen. Here, Tom will not be able to sue Harry for the money, as he has given no consideration for his promise. If, however, Dick does the work for Harry, Dick will be able to sue Harry and force him to pay Tom. Likewise, if Harry paid Tom, he would be able to sue Dick in an attempt to force him to paint the kitchen.

It may be difficult to see what consideration Dick has received for his promise to do the work for Harry, and that brings up another rule. The courts will not inquire into the adequacy of the consideration given as long as some value can be attached to it. Therefore, in the above example, the courts would assume that the payment by Harry to Tom had a definite value to Dick, and, once these elements are present, the courts will not try to weigh the values against each other.

This, however, must not be confused with a situation where no value or consideration is given at all. Assume Tom owed Dick $100 to be repaid on April 1. Suppose that on April 1 Tom contacts Dick and says, "April fool... I will repay my debt to you today only if you agree to accept $50 in full satisfaction of my debt." Here, there is no valid consideration, as the repayment of the debt is already something that Tom is legally bound to. However, if Tom had contacted Harry on February 1 and had said, "I will agree to pay you $50 at this time if you will agree to accept it in full satisfaction of the debt of $100 which is not due until April 1," the consideration would have been the early payment of the debt.

3. Legal capacity

To be able to enter into a contractual relationship, the parties to the contract must have legal capacity (i.e., a capacity to enter into a legally binding contract). Unless a party has legal capacity, the courts will not enforce a contract against such a party.

(a) An insane person does not have legal capacity. However, it may be difficult to determine whether a person is mentally disordered to the extent that the courts will not enforce a contract against that person. However, if this person is declared to be insane, he or she will not be held to be bound by a contract.

(b) An "infant" in British Columbia is a person who is under the age of 19 years. Such a person cannot be bound by a contract unless the contract is for necessaries.

Necessaries are not confined to articles necessary to the support of life, but include articles and services required to maintain that particular "infant" in his or her station of life at the time. That could conceivably include the purchase of real estate, and problems can occur in relation to an "infant" buying land in British Columbia.

(c) A person who is under the influence of alcohol or, perhaps, drugs will not be held to be obligated to the other party to the contract if it can be shown that —

(i) that person was incapable of understanding, and

(ii) the other person knew about the condition.

(d) A company may also be unable to enter into a contract unless all of the matters pertaining to the contract are within its powers. These powers are usually either laid down by statute or in the company's incorporation documents. If a company exceeds its powers, the courts may decide that the company had no capacity to enter into the contract.

4. Lawful object

A contract to do an illegal act cannot be sued on and therefore cannot be enforced. An example of this would be hiring someone to steal. This is a public policy decision that the courts made a long time ago.

5. Intention to create legal and enforceable obligations

The parties to a contract must intend to be bound by the agreement and by the legal consequences if it is breached. If the parties were to enter into a contract as a joke, the court would not enforce the contract.

The previous sections in this chapter have dealt with the elements required to form a contract. When all such elements are present and the parties believe they have entered into a contract, they should be entitled to rely on the courts to enforce such a contract.

The next couple of sections deal very briefly with circumstances that could upset such expectations and with the remedies that would be available under such circumstances. For easy discussion, the circumstances can be divided under three headings: unenforceable contracts, voidable contracts, and void contracts.

c. UNENFORCEABLE CONTRACTS

The unenforceable contract is a contract that cannot successfully be sued on to enforce it. However, what has already been done according to a contract remains effective and cannot be upset.

Many people believe that for a contract to be valid it must be in writing. This is simply not true, although there could be a problem proving the contents of an oral agreement. Nevertheless, contracts concerning a guarantee, indemnity, or an

22

interest in land *must be in writing* to be enforceable. This is because of the B.C. Statute of Frauds.

Take, for instance, the situation where Mr. I. Cheete decided to lease a lush penthouse apartment as his bachelor pad for five years. His landlady, Mrs. E. Vict, agreed to grant him such a lease provided that Mr. Cheete's rich uncle, D.B.L. Cross, would guarantee the payment of the rent. All parties agreed to this arrangement verbally and nothing was put in writing then or later. All parties abided by their contract until six months later when Cheete, who was disenchanted with his bachelor suite, moved out of his penthouse in the dark of night without giving notice or paying his rent. Naturally Mrs. E. Vict was very upset and consulted her lawyer to see if she could sue either or both Cheete and D.B.L. Cross. Her lawyer, Mr. Knowitall, advised her that in all likelihood she would —

(a) be successful on a claim for back rent, because even though a lease is a contract concerning an interest in land and, therefore, should be in writing, the services had been performed and it had now become a matter of payment for services rendered;

(b) lose on a claim against the uncle, as the guarantee was not in writing — as required by the Statute of Frauds; and

(c) lose on a claim for further damages (for loss of future rent under the lease) as this was a contract concerning an interest in land and, therefore, had to be in writing to be enforceable — as required by the Statute of Frauds.

As it can be seen, in any contract concerning an interest in land, the Statute of Frauds should always be complied with and the contract should be in writing. To comply, it must —

(a) identify the parties to the contract,

(b) contain the terms of the agreement sufficiently, and

23

(c) be signed by the person sought to be held liable (i.e., it is only necessary to have a guarantee signed by the person giving the guarantee. The person to whom the guarantee was granted need not sign.)

d. VOIDABLE CONTRACTS

If someone is induced to enter into a contract by a misrepresentation, whether it is innocent or fraudulent, this misrepresentation renders a contract voidable. A person who has been induced to enter into a contract on the basis of an innocent misrepresentation may take steps to avoid the contract but cannot generally recover damages. However, a person who is induced to enter into the contract by a fraudulent misrepresentation can generally not only void the contract but also recover damages.

An example of this would be where Gail Gasser decides to buy, for instance, a service station from A. Weasel. The gas station is located on a busy main thoroughfare, but Weasel knows that a bypass road is being constructed which will serve to divert the traffic away from the gas station.

Gail Gasser would not be able to void the contract unless Weasel had told her that he knew of nothing that would affect the traffic flow. Such a statement would amount to fraudulent misrepresentation. Even if a contract is induced by fraud, the contract is not automatically cancelled, but is only liable to be cancelled (voidable) at the option of the deceived party.

Contracts can also be voidable where one party has exerted excessive duress or undue influence on the other party.

e. CONTRACTS THAT ARE VOID

The term "void contract" is really a paradox since a contract that is void means that it was void from its inception and, consequently, that the contract never came into being. The following are examples of void contracts.

1. By mistake

This contract is void because it lacks one of the essential elements of a contract, namely that of mutual agreement. Take for instance the situation where an offer is made by Michael to sell a "Picasso" to Angelo, and Angelo accepts Michael's offer without any qualification or reservation. Both Michael and Angelo honestly believe the painting to be a genuine Picasso. Later, when it is discovered that the picture is not a Picasso, the whole transaction falls apart, as the subject of the transaction was something other than what both parties had contemplated.

When the contract has been completed, the courts will attempt to put the parties back to where they were before the transaction was entered into. The same would apply if, for instance, Michael knew that he was selling an imitation Picasso, but through no fault of Michael's, Angelo was under the impression that he was buying a real Picasso.

Another example of a mistake is where X orally agrees to sell a house, excluding an adjoining yard, to Y. Due to a mistake, the conveyancing documentation includes the yard as part of the property that is being sold, and, what is even worse, the actual resignation of the conveyance conveys the yard to Y. In such a situation, the court will not only rectify the simply written documentation, but will also order that the yard be conveyed back to X.

2. By statute

If certain contracts are prohibited by statute, they are void. Statute includes all acts, orders, rules, and regulations that are authorized or laid down by the government. One such example, until recently, was the Canada-wide, antiquated Lord's Day Act, which had the effect (until ruled unconstitutional by the Supreme Court of Canada) of making void under certain circumstances a contract made on a Sunday (including, for example, an interim agreement). Likewise, the Statute of Frauds which was enacted in England in 1677 and remained part of the law in British Columbia until 1985, provided that contracts dealing with land could not be enforced without being in writing and bearing the signature of at least the party trying to avoid the contract. Although a contract dealing with land must still be in writing if it is to be enforceable, other parts of the old Statute of Frauds have been changed by the Law and Equity Act.

3. On grounds of public policy

These contracts exclude contracts to commit a crime, contracts that are sexually immoral, contracts that will prejudice public safety, contracts that are prejudicial to the administration of justice, contracts that will promote corruption in public life, or contracts that will restrain trade.

f. BREACH OF CONTRACT

If one enters a contract and deliberately violates it, the injured party has a "right of action," which provides the injured party with access to the courts. The courts will then attempt to remedy the breach. The type of remedy that is available will depend on the circumstances.

When the nature of the breach is so important to the contract that the other party would be getting something completely different from that bargained for, such a breach would allow the injured party to treat the contract as over, and the injured party would, therefore, be discharged from any further obligation.

In addition, the injured party could sue for damages occasioned by the breach or, in certain instances, hold the defaulter to the promise (specific performance), or both.

In an action for specific performance, the court will be asked to enforce the specific terms of the contract. Injured parties who select this avenue, of course, are also bound to complete their end of the contract, if they have not already done so.

If the breach is of a minor nature, it is referred to as a breach of warranty and gives the injured party a right to damage only.

As you have probably gathered by now, a contract is very complicated. It is not the purpose of this book to provide a detailed study of contract law but only to give a very superficial introduction to the subject of contracts. A person involved in a breach of contract situation should seek professional help, for not only are the types of breaches of contract complicated, but so are the remedies available. It may cost money to seek professional guidance, but it could cost more if such guidance is not obtained.

Needless to say, a purchaser of property who refuses to complete a purchase of real estate could become liable to the vendor for any deficiency in price arising on a further sale to another party. Similarly, a vendor of property who refuses to complete a sale of real estate could become liable for damages resulting to the purchaser from such a refusal. In addition, problems such as tender of purchase money or conveyancing documentation must be dealt with by a professional, as such actions could decide the ultimate outcome of the case.

g. REPRESENTATIONS AND WARRANTIES

This has been touched on to some extent in the previous sections, but a few additional items should be mentioned.

In British Columbia, the general principle of law is that in the case of a sale of real estate where there is no fraud, the purchaser has no grounds for complaint if a defect in quality is found in the house later. Two exceptions to this rule are the following:

(a) The defect affects the title given by the vendor.

(b) The vendor promised that the property had the quality now found to be missing.

27

In fact, the law is clear that there is no implied warranty that a residential property should even be fit for habitation! Therefore, to protect yourself when buying a home, ask many questions and insist upon obtaining the answers before submitting an offer to purchase. For items that are of particular importance, the vendor should be requested to make, in the offer, written warranties and representations based on these answers (see chapter 3, section **d.**).

The situation is different for new homes. Here the law varies, depending upon whether the agreement is to have a house built, to purchase a partially completed house, or to purchase a house already completed.

If you are having a house built, you should, of course, have a contract drawn between you and the builder setting out all the terms and conditions. This way you can obtain as much or as little protection as you want.

Even if the contract does not make reference to plans and specifications, there is an implied warranty (the breach of which entitles the innocent party to damages only) that the home is fit for human habitation and that the materials used are reasonably adequate for the purposes for which they are used. On the other hand, where reference is made to plans and specifications, you (the person who is having the house built) may lose your right of action as long as the builder builds to the express terms of the contract, even if the plans are faulty.

If you are purchasing a partially completed house, the law appears to imply that there is a warranty for the work done both before and after the purchase contract is entered into. Basically, the law here is the same as that for having a house built.

If, however, the house has been completed by the time the contract to purchase is signed, it appears that the only way you can protect yourself is to obtain an express written warranty from the vendor. There is no implied warranty of fitness for human habitation and it is "caveat emptor" all the way.

h. CONCLUSION

Again, I would like to repeat that this discussion of contracts is very superficial. It is intended only to introduce you briefly to contract law so that you will be able to understand and appreciate the legal significance of the interim agreement and the importance of seeking professional guidance if you are uncertain or if you encounter difficulties.

3
HOW TO ACTUALLY SELECT AND BUY A HOME

a. BE PREPARED TO PUT IN A LOT OF EFFORT

Once you have determined the price range, you can actually start looking for a home. This can be hard work and should not be taken lightly. How many homes should you view before making a decision? The industry average seems to be eight. This is far too low a number. Three times that number should be the minimum. It would increase your knowledge and perception about the housing market immeasurably. If you think about it, many ideas you have about the kind of home you want come from the direct viewing of other homes. So it stands to reason, the more you get to look at, the better your chance of getting one to suit you.

As mentioned previously, a home is probably the biggest investment of most people's lives, and any errors involved in the purchase can be costly. First, decide what you require in housing and what you can realistically expect to obtain in your price range. Second, decide the general area in which the house should be located. Third, attempt to obtain some feel for what is available in the general area.

Become familiar with price structure. There are a number of ways of doing this, such as by looking through newspaper advertisements and publications offering homes for sale or attending open houses. Going to open houses is one of the best ways (although time-consuming) to obtain the experience to enable you to judge and select a good buy, rather than a poor one without relying entirely on an agent's advice.

Sample #1 is a checklist of many of the factors you should consider.

Also become familiar with the market for financing the house. Is it a buyer's market to the extent that sellers are prepared to carry financing? How much mortgage money is generally available at banks and trust companies? On what terms?

b. THE REAL ESTATE SALESPERSON OR AGENT

By far the majority of homes are purchased through a real estate agent. Contact with an agent is most often made through an advertisement in the paper, by going to an agent's office to inquire about a house, or by attending an open house.

As is the same in any profession, the ability of real estate agents varies from individual to individual. The good, knowledgeable, and helpful real estate agent can be a tremendous asset both to a vendor and a purchaser. Therefore, if it is at all possible, attempt to get the best agent available either through a recommendation or by meeting a few and then selecting the one who suits your needs best.

When looking for an agent, try to select one who deals exclusively with houses in the area in which you are interested in settling. Some agents deal only with commercial or industrial real estate and some restrict their activities to limited geographical areas. This is especially so in the larger urban centres. An agent will help you locate the house that is most suitable for you and negotiate with the vendor over price, terms, etc. An agent also usually writes the offer to purchase or interim agreement, and, therefore, should have a basic knowledge of real estate law.

Just because a particular house is listed with a certain real estate company does not necessarily mean that a prospective buyer has to contact that particular company. The purchaser can choose to contact any agent he or she wishes.

SAMPLE #1
CHECKLIST FOR THE HOUSE BUYER

Address: _____

SITE DATA: Lot Size _____ x _____

SERVICES	
Water	
Gas	
Sanitary Sewer	
Septic Tank	
Storm Sewers	

ROAD TYPE	
Paved	
Gravel	
Curbs	
Sidewalks	

LANDSCAPING	
Good	
Fair	
Poor	

SIZE OF LOT FOR AREA	
Large	
Average	
Small	

TYPE	
Detached	
Semi-Detached	
No. of Storeys	
Split	

EXTERIOR	
Brick	
Stone	
Siding	
Stucco	

ROOF	
Asphalt/Duroid	
Cedar	
Slate	
Tar & Gravel	

PARKING – Capacity	
Garage	
Carport	
None	

DRIVEWAY	
Private	
Mutual	
Lane	

FLOOR PLAN	
Good	
Fair	
Poor	
Main Floor Area	sq. ft.

INTERIOR WALLS	
Plaster	
Dry Wall	
Panelling	

BASEMENT	
Full	
Partial	
None-Slab	
None-Crawl	

HEATING SYSTEM	
Hot Water	
Gravity Air	
Forced Air	
Electrical	

FUEL	
Coal	
Oil	
Gas	
Conversion	

MAINTENANCE	
Excellent	
Good	
Fair	
Poor	

lumbing, repairing the leak in the
attending to the garden, and so on.

ew home. As a matter of fact, some
re time-consuming, as they usually
landscaping to be completed. This
oked by people purchasing a home,
people who do not have enough time
find the experience very frustrating.
tter off owning a townhouse where
ning chores are done for them.

cost of housing is difficult. Mass pro-
uilder money, and some of these sav-
to the purchaser. Mass production in
ver, also means that a builder is limited
of styles of homes. This, unfortunately,
tion for the purchaser.

omes either from model homes or from
ons, a builder can save additional money
is already sold, the transaction can be
as the house is finished; thus the builder
to pay the carrying charges from the time
the time it is sold. On a large project this
erable saving. It also allows the purchaser
lors of carpets, bathroom fixtures, etc. Fur-
by the builder can be obtained since more
cts can be negotiated with suppliers and
negotiating with volume.

our alternatives are somewhat limited when
mass-produced home, some choices are still
e you have decided on the model, you are
choose, from a limited number, the color of the
or the interior, and the color of the bathroom
ets, etc. Any further changes or additional items
vailable and even if they are, they will be "extras"
e cost will be added on to the purchase price.

FIREPLACE	INSULATION	WIRING		HOT WATER	PLUMBING	FLOORS
Open	Walls	Amp. 60	100	Electric	Galvanized	Hardwood
Electric	Ceiling	New		Gas	Copper	Tile
Gas	Roof	Old		Oil	Plastic	Carpet
None		Adequate		Capacity		

Number and Type of Rooms

	L/R	D/R	Kit.	BATH	WASH	FAM.	OTHER
Basement							
1st Floor							
2nd Floor							
Other							

KITCHEN	BATHROOM	LIVING ROOM	BEDROOMS	CLOSETS
Excellent	New	Excellent	Large	Ample
Good	Average	Good	Medium	Adequate
Fair	Fair	Fair	Small	Fair
Poor	Outdated	Poor		Inadequate

Most agents cooperate with one another to the extent that an agent from A company who has a purchaser can approach the agent from B company who has the listing so that arrangements can be made to show the property to the prospective purchaser and, if the purchaser is interested enough, to present an offer to the vendor. The real estate agents will, in this instance, split the commission if there is a sale.

In many cases, this is a more comfortable situation for both the purchaser and the vendor, as theoretically, both parties will have an agent representing their interests, although legally both are agents of the vendor, who customarily pays the commission.

Since the agent who has the listing is paid on commission and by the vendor, that agent will try to secure the highest price possible while keeping in mind that it is better to sell a house at a lower price than not to sell it at all.

Most agents are also members of a multiple listing service, which is a cooperative service among real estate agents that disseminates listing information to its members. This not only gives the listing a larger exposure, but also provides prospective purchasers with a larger selection. Such listings are given on listing sheets that usually contain a picture of each house and its specifications, such as the number of bathrooms, number of bedrooms, number of fireplaces, and square footage of the house. These enable prospective purchasers to narrow down their choices in the comfort of the real estate agent's office rather than having to invest the time and effort to actually inspect each house.

Before you even approach an agent, you should have some idea of what you want. Then the agent can immediately select the homes that meet these criteria rather than using the time-consuming method of trial and error which wastes time for everyone concerned. When you find "the one," try to make several inspections of the house prior to making the offer, so that the house can be seen both in the daytime and at night.

Reference to all color choices made and extras required should be included either in the interim agreement itself or in a schedule attached to the interim agreement. The same applies where the builder agrees to any out-of-the-ordinary deviations — for example, if certain appliances that you want are not available from the builder as the regular appliances and have to be installed as extras by the builder. The builder may, however, be prepared to give you an "appliance credit" on the purchase price and then not install any appliances whatsoever. Then you will be able to obtain your own appliances and have them installed. There are, of course, an unlimited number of such deviations and they should be included in the interim agreement to protect both parties.

Another area in which you may have a limited choice is in the mortgage financing. Many builders arrange their construction financing in such a way that, on completion of the house, such financing becomes a conventional mortgage to be assumed by the purchaser. This could be a disadvantage to you if the mortgage financing does not fit your requirements.

On the other hand, it could be an advantage, as you would be spared the ordeal of searching for financing of your own and paying the costs incurred in connection with obtaining such financing. These costs could include fees for an appraisal, a survey certificate, and the legal documentation, to mention some of the most common.

If the financing does not suit your needs, the builder may not be prepared to sell the house since the mortgage company may not be prepared to accept payment of the mortgage prematurely, or, even if it would, the builder may not be prepared to absorb the prepayment penalty that the mortgage company assesses in these cases.

2. Completion and moving dates

One of the main problems that you will encounter when purchasing a home that is not yet completed is that of coordinating the completion date of the home with your occupation date. If this is not done properly, two problems can occur.

First, you usually have to make arrangements to move well in advance of the scheduled possession date and have probably either sold your home with a similar possession date or given up your lease. You then find that you have to move but have no place to move to, as the new home is not yet completed.

Second, if you choose to take possession of the house even though it is uncompleted because you have nowhere else to go, the builder will probably insist that the entire purchase price be paid before you are allowed to move in. You then will have to depend on the builder's continued financial solvency and integrity to complete the remaining items of construction in a good and professional manner and within a reasonable period of time. This can cause major problems for you.

Suppose, for example, there are several items of construction that must be completed after you have paid your money, but the builder, before being able to complete them, goes into bankruptcy. In this situation, you are faced with the problem of having to get another contractor to do the first contractor's work and, in essence, you end up paying two people to do the same job.

To compound the problem even more, many builders' forms of interim agreements contain a clause in which the purchaser agrees to take possession of the dwelling, as long as it is "habitable," and pay the entire balance on that date. (Sample #2 is an example of one form of an offer to purchase a new house. Remember, once accepted, the offer to purchase becomes the interim agreement — a binding contract.)

To avoid problems, you should consider the following:

(a) When the possession date (date you can move in) and the completion date (date your money is paid to the seller) are discussed for drawing up the interim agreement, get an estimate from the builder as to when the

38

SAMPLE #2
INTERIM AGREEMENT (NEW HOUSE)

INTERIM AGREEMENT
(British Columbia)

THIS OFFER to enter into a binding contract of purchase and sale is made this _____5th_____ day
(insert date)

of _____January_____, 19 9- by_____
(insert date) *(insert names of buyers)*

_____Bill Hinton and Jennifer Towers_____

(hereinafter called the "Purchaser") having an address of _____275 Washington Way_____
(insert civic address)

_____Delta_____ _____B.C._____ _____ _____
(municipality) *(province)* *(postal code)* *(telephone number)*

The Purchaser, having inspected the real property described as _____50 Cessna Crescent_____
(civic address)

_____ Surrey, B.C. _____
(municipality)

having a legal description of _____Lot 1, Block 23, Section 5, District Lot 456,_____
(insert legal description)

_____Plan 7890, N.W.D._____

(the "Property") on the _____5th_____ day of _____January_____, 19 9- hereby

offers to purchase the Property from the owners thereof (hereinafter called the "Vendor") for the

price and on the terms and subject to the conditions herein set forth, namely:

1. PURCHASE PRICE: The purchase price shall be _Two Hundred and Twenty-Five_

_Thousand_____ Dollars ($ _225,000.00_____) payable as follows:

    a.   Paid as a deposit by   ☐   ☒
                           (cash) *(cheque)*

       the sum of: $ _____1,000_____

    b.   Cash on completion $ _____49,000_____

    c.   Balance, if any, as indicated below in the amount of $ _____175,000_____

       TOTAL: $ _____225,000_____

Balance, if any, as per paragraph c. above shall be paid as follows:

Assumption of First Mortgage as per Schedule "A" - $150,000

By Second Mortgage to Vendor as per Schedule "A" - $ 25,000
                                              $175,000

2. TITLE: The title shall be free and clear of all encumbrances except existing restrictions, exceptions and conditions reserved in favor of the Crown, registered restrictive covenants and rights of way in favor of utilities and public authorities, statutory building schemes, building, zoning and other municipal or governmental restrictions, the existing tenancies specified below, if any, and any other exceptions set out herein. If the Vendor has existing financial encumbrances to clear from the title, the Vendor may wait to pay and discharge such until immediately after receipt of the sales proceeds (provided such is sufficient). In such event, however, the Purchaser shall pay the sales proceeds to a lawyer or notary in trust, on undertakings to pay and discharge the financial encumbrances, and the balance if any, shall be paid to the Vendor.

3. COMPLETION: The sale shall be completed on or before the _____27th_____ day of _____February_____, 19 9- _____ (the Completion Date) at the appropriate Land Title Office. Tender or payment of monies by the Purchaser to the Vendor shall be by certified cheque, bank draft, or lawyer's or notary's trust cheque. All documents required to give effect to this contract shall be delivered on or before the Completion Date and shall be, where necessary, in a form acceptable for registration in the appropriate Land Title Office. Time is of the essence and unless the balance of the cash payment is paid and such formal agreement to pay the balance as may be necessary is entered into on or before the Completion Date, the Vendor may, at the Vendor's option, terminate this contract and in such event the amount paid by the Purchaser will be absolutely forfeited to the Vendor on account of damages, without prejudice to the Vendor's other remedies. If the Purchaser is relying upon a new mortgage to finance the purchase of the Property, the Purchaser, while still required to pay the Purchase Price on the Completion Date, may wait to pay the net proceeds of such mortgage to the Purchaser's solicitor until after the transfer and new mortgage documents have been lodged for registration in the appropriate Land Title Office, but only if, before such lodging, the Purchaser has: a) made available to the Vendor that portion of the Purchase Price due on completion less the net proceeds of the new mortgage, and b) fulfilled all the new mortgagee's conditions for funding except lodging of the mortgage for registration, and c) made available to the Vendor a lawyer's or notary's undertaking to pay the balance due on completion upon the lodging of the transfer and new mortgage documents and the advance by the mortgagee of the mortgage proceeds.

4. ADJUSTMENTS: The Purchaser will assume and pay all taxes, rates, local improvement assessments, fuel, utilities and other charges from and including the ____1st____ day of ____March____ 19_9_ (the "Adjustment Date") from which date all adjustments both incoming and outgoing of whatsoever nature will be made and the Vendor shall pay all such charges to such date. The balance of the Purchase Price due on Completion shall reflect such Adjustments.

5. COSTS: The Purchaser will bear all costs of the conveyance, and, if applicable, the costs related to arranging a mortgage and the Vendor will bear all costs of clearing title.

6. POSSESSION: The Purchaser will have vacant possession of the Property at 12:00 noon on the ____1st____ day of ____March____ 19_9_ (the "Possession Date") such possession to be a) vacant ☐ or b) subject to the following existing tenancies:

____Tenancy to Tina Tenant as per Schedule "A"____

7. RISK: All the buildings on the Property and all other items included in the Purchase Price will be and remain at the risk of the Vendor until 12:01 a.m. on the Completion Date. After that time, the Property and all included items will be at the risk of the Purchaser. In the event that the building or other items included in the purchase and sale are destroyed or substantially damaged prior to Completion, the Purchaser shall elect prior to the Completion Date by notice in writing either to terminate this agreement and have the deposit together with any accrued interest returned or to complete the purchase with the benefit of any insurance proceeds to be for the account of the Purchaser.

8. INCLUDED ITEMS: The Purchase Price includes any buildings, improvements, fixtures, appurtenances and attachments thereto and all blinds, awnings, screen doors and windows, curtain rods, tracks and valences, fixed mirrors, fixed carpeting, electric, plumbing, heating and air conditioning fixtures and all appurtenances and attachments thereto as viewed by the Purchaser at the date of inspection including

____Washer, dryer, refrigerator and stove____

but excluding ____chandelier in dining room which Vendor may remove____

The Property and all included items shall be in substantially the same condition at the Possession Date as when viewed by the Purchaser on the Inspection date.

9. CONDITIONS: In addition to all other conditions contained herein, the Purchaser is submitting this offer on the following express conditions, which conditions the Vendor by accepting this offer warrants and represents to be true, namely:

  a. The Property has been used only as a residential property by the Vendor until the date of sale and is exempt from the payment of GST on sale;

  b. The Vendor is not now nor will 60 days after the Possession Date be a non-resident of Canada within the meaning of the Income Tax Act of Canada nor is the Vendor the agent or trustee for anyone with an interest in this property who is or will, 60 days from the Possession Date, be a non-resident of Canada within the meaning of the Income Tax Act of Canada.

  c. The attached Property Condition Disclosure Statement dated the ____5th____ day of ____January____, 19_9_ is true and correct and is incorporated into this contract and forms an integral part thereof.

  d. The Property has ☐ has not ☒ been insulated with urea formaldehyde.

  e. Other ____see Schedule "A" attached hereto which forms____

  ____part of this Interim Agreement.____

SAMPLE #2 — Continued

f.   Each condition contained in this agreement is for the sole benefit of the party indicated, where so indicated and unless each condition is waived or declared fulfilled by written notice given by the benefiting party to the other party on or before the date specified for each condition, this contract will thereupon be terminated and any deposit paid hereunder shall be immediately returned.

10.   GENERAL:

a.   There are no warranties, representations, guarantees, promises, or agreements other than those set out herein, all of which shall survive the completion of the sale.

b.   Any reference to a party in this contract includes that party's heirs, executors, administrators, and assigns and the singular includes the plural and the feminine includes the masculine.

11.   TIME FOR ACCEPTANCE: This offer (or counter-offer as the case may be) is open for acceptance until ___6:00___ o'clock __P__ m on the __8th__ day of ___January___ 19_9-_

and upon acceptance thereof in writing with notification to the other party of such acceptance.

THIS CONTRACT SHALL BE A BINDING CONTRACT OF PURCHASE AND SALE ON THE TERMS AND CONDITIONS SET OUT HEREIN.

Bill Hinton	Bill Hinton	_[signature]_
Purchaser	Print name	Witness
Jennifer Towers	Jennifer Towers	_[signature]_
Purchaser	Print name	Witness

THE VENDOR HEREBY ACCEPTS THE ABOVE OFFER THIS ___7th___ DAY OF

___January___, 19_9-_, acknowledges receipt of the deposit, and agrees to complete the sale on the terms and conditions set out herein.

Freddy Flight	Freddy Flight	_A. Friend_
Vendor	Print name	Witness

_____	_____	_____
Vendor	Print name	Witness

___50 Cessna Crescent, Surrey, B.C.___
Vendor's address

___535-9991___	___246-AWAY___
Home phone	Work phone

CONVEYANCING INFORMATION:

___Diane Lawyer___	___681-0123___
Name of purchaser's lawyer/notary Phone	

___1234 - 5th Street, Vancouver, B.C. V1A 3Z2___
Address

___Rich Slickenfast___	___246-8010___
Name of vendor's lawyer/notary	Phone

___999 Golden Brick Lane, Vancouver, B.C.___
Address

SCHEDULE "A"

To the Interim Agreement dated January 5, 199- wherein Bill Hinton and Jennifer Towers are "Purchaser" of the property known as 50 Cessna Crescent, Surrey, B.C.

1.   The details of the mortgages referred to in paragraph 1, page 1 of this Interim Agreement are as follows:

a.   The Purchasers shall assume the existing First Mortgage in favour of Friendly Trust Company having a balance of approximately $150,000.00 bearing interest at 9 1/2% per annum calculated half yearly, not in advance, being repayable in equal monthly blended instalments of $1,377.70 (principal and interest only) maturing October 31, 199- and containing no prepayment privileges.

b.   The sum of $25,000.00 by way of a Second Mortgage to the Vendor, such Mortgage to bear interest at the rate of 9% per annum, calculated half yearly, not in advance, being repayable in equal blended monthly instalments of $207.00 on the 1st day of each and every month during the term commencing on March 1, 199- and maturing on October 31, 199- and containing a privilege whereby the Purchasers may prepay the whole or any part of the principal at any time or times without notice, penalty or bonus.

2.   The Vendor covenants and agrees as follows:

(a)   That he will at his cost provide to the Purchaser or their solicitor a survey certificate of the real property, within fifteen (15) days of the date of acceptance hereof, which survey certificate shall show the location of all buildings and rights-of-way and easements of the property relative to the property lines;

(b)   That the Purchaser shall have the right to inspect the real property during daylight hours until the closing of the within transaction, upon providing to the Vendor 24 hours prior notice of their intention to inspect;

(c)   The property has been used only as a residential property by the Vendor until the date of sale and is exempt from the payment of GST on sale.

3. The following are conditions for the completion of the within transaction by the Purchaser, which conditions are for the benefit of the Purchaser only and may be waived by them in writing at any time hereafter:

(a) The dwelling on the real property being purchased has been constructed in accordance with and presently complies with all relevant municipal, provincial, and federal requirements and that fences and buildings are within the property lines;

(b) The heating system, plumbing system, electrical system and roof are not in need of repair. The Purchasers shall have the right to have. the plumbing system, heating system, electrical system and roof inspected by their agents or contractors prior to January 15, 199- and such inspection shall be satisfactory to the Purchaser or they may, on or prior to that date, at their election cancel this agreement and have their money refunded;

(c) There are no easements, rights-of-way or encroachments of any kind whatsoever affecting the real property, save and except for an easement in favour of B.C. Hydro which easement is located along the rear ten feet of the said property;

(d) That the upstairs suite of the dwelling is rented to Tina Tenant on a month-to-month tenancy at a rent of $400.00 per month, payable in advance, on the 1st day of each and every month; that the said suite is a legal suite and that the rent has not been increased since May 1, 199-.

building is expected to be ready and then add to that date 30 days, or as long a period as you may feel is reasonable, and try to get the builder to accept the new date. (This will allow for some margin of error.)

(b) Provide in the interim agreement that it is a condition by you that the house be fully completed by the completion date; otherwise you shall have the option of *one* of the following:

(i) Postponing the completion date until the house is fully complete.

(ii) Agreeing with the builder on the outstanding items in writing and, based on such items, agreeing to an appropriate amount of money to hold back until such items have been completed. This amount could be held in trust by either the builder's or purchaser's lawyer and not released until the lawyer receives permission from both parties or is given satisfactory proof that the items agreed upon have been completed.

Depending on the market conditions and the builder, there may or may not be any room for negotiations. Many builders have had their interim agreements specially prepared to suit their circumstances and feel that the prospective purchasers must either accept or reject that form. Here it can only be suggested that if you ask for something that is reasonable and the builder is not obliging, it may very well be your first warning of storm clouds ahead — so watch out!

3. Contracting to build a new home

Instead of buying a home from a builder, you may wish to have a home built to your specifications. Should this be the case, you should choose the contractor carefully and give considerable thought to that contractor's reputation.

A construction agreement is of paramount importance, but it should be remembered that a contract is only as good as the people who make it. Ideally, a construction contract should be tailor-made to a specific job in order to cover specifically what must be done. However, the following elements are common to most construction contracts. Give some thought to them before you enter into discussions with a builder.

(a) The date of the agreement and an accurate definition of the parties

(b) An accurate description of the work to be done by the contractor

(c) The time of commencement and completion of the work

(d) Damages in case the completion date is not met (This should be an honest estimate of the damages; otherwise it will not stand up in court.)

(e) The price and terms of payment

(f) Consideration of a performance bond

(g) Warranties that the work will be performed in a competent manner and that all materials will be new

(h) Clarification of whose responsibility it shall be to pay for and obtain permits, licences, and connection fees

(i) Particulars of fire and liability insurance to be carried on the project

(j) Provision for the contractor to obtain written approval by the owner before extra costs are incurred and additional work is done

(k) Provisions to correct and remedy defects in workmanship and material for a certain period of time, as well as a provision setting out the owner's alternative in the event of a breach of contract

(l) A provision by the builder to protect the owner against mechanics' lien claims

(m) A provision that the builder and that builder's sub-trades abide by all laws

(n) A provision requiring the contractor to clean up after the job is completed

(o) A provision for settling disputes by arbitration (optional)

(p) A standard provision stating that the contract contains the entire agreement unless altered in writing

(q) A provision stating how a notice is to be given to the parties under the contract should it be required

(r) A provision indicating the agreement is binding on the heirs and successors of the parties

It is absolutely essential that both parties, the buyer as well as the builder, understand exactly what is expected of them. Disputes can be very costly and extremely aggravating. To reduce the chance of a legal dispute, the Canadian Home Builders Association of B.C. has printed a series of standard construction contracts. These include not only new house sales contracts, but also renovation agreements, change-order forms, and builder/sub-contractor agreements, and can be purchased for a small fee. Telephone the association at 432-7112 for more information. You can also write to the association at the address below:

Canadian Home Builders Association of B.C.
3700 Willingdon Avenue
Burnaby, B.C.
V5G 3H2

4. Builders Lien Act

A builder's lien applies to contractors, sub-contractors, and material suppliers.

Therefore, the Builders Lien Act of British Columbia is a very important consideration for anybody purchasing a new home, doing additional construction, or renovating.

The Builders Lien Act *obliges* an owner to withhold from the contractor 10% of the contract price (or fair market value) *of the improvements* put on the land until 40 days have elapsed after completion or abandonment of the contract.

In the case of a strata title property such as condominiums and townhouses such holdback is 7% of the *total purchase price.* An owner who breaches this requirement can be liable for the amount not held back. This is over and above the amount provided for in the building contract.

Although it is a statutory requirement, it is recommended that a provision also be made in the interim agreement stipulating that you, the purchaser, reserve the right to retain the builder's lien holdback from the purchase price for 40 days following completion. When this period has expired, you or somebody on your behalf should make a search in the Land Title Office to make sure that the property is free of liens before paying out the final lien holdback.

If there are liens registered, contact your lawyer to make sure these liens are discharged before you pay out any money. Similarly, you should be aware of the fact that if there are liens registered against a property, a mortgage company will not make progress advances until these liens are lifted.

There are a number of ways of having builders' liens discharged from a property but it is impossible to fully discuss all the aspects of the Builders Lien Act in this book. Needless to say, if you are ever involved in a situation where a builder's lien has been filed against your home, you should seek professional guidance immediately.

5. Occupancy certificate

Most municipalities have bylaws that make it illegal to occupy a new home until an occupancy certificate has been issued. Most such bylaws impose a penalty not only upon the builder but also upon the people who have taken occupancy illegally. A person should, therefore, ensure that the occupancy certificate has been issued before moving into a new house. This can be easily verified by contacting the appropriate municipal authority, or by having the certificate delivered by the builder before the transaction closes.

6. Land use and zoning

The purpose of zoning bylaws is to govern the orderly development of the community. The zoning bylaws regulate and govern, among other things, the use the building may be put to, the type of building that may be constructed, and the set back — that is, the required distance between the house and the lot lines.

Such regulations provide that all homes in the area will conform to the planning principles laid down by the municipal authorities. Again, if you are in doubt about whether the home being purchased, new or old, conforms to the local zoning bylaws, you can easily verify it by contacting the appropriate municipal authorities. This should be done especially if any alterations or additions to the home are planned.

Municipal councils have, under the Municipal Act, power to provide any zoning bylaw or amendment for issuance of "development permits." Therefore, as a land owner, you have the option of developing your property under the existing zoning bylaws and regulations or by applying for a development permit. The latter would allow you greater flexibility in certain instances, but would in all likelihood also include additional requirements dictated by council.

Under the development permit system, council may regulate the size, shape, and siting of buildings, offstreet parking, loading facilities, landscaping, pavement of roads and parking areas, requirements for sewage, water, and drainage facilities; provide special requirements for construction of buildings; regulate the exterior finishing of buildings, signs, etc.; and provide for recreation and play areas.

The development permit may not, however, allow a change in the land use or density as described in the zoning bylaw. Accordingly, the issuance of a development permit does not require a public hearing, whereas a change in zoning would.

7. The real estate prospectus

The Real Estate Act of British Columbia is divided into two parts. The first part deals basically with real estate agents, salespeople, and licencees; the second part deals exclusively with subdivisions. The second part of the act also imposes an obligation upon the promoter of the land to file a real estate prospectus with the office of the Superintendent of Insurance.

The real estate prospectus requirements apply to any land to be divided into five or more parcels or lots for the purposes of sale or lease whether that is done by normal subdivision or under the Strata Title Act or through a cooperative or time share plan.

Once the prospectus has been filed and accepted by the Superintendent, the property can be offered for sale, but not before then. The act also requires that every purchaser receive a copy of the prospectus and be given an opportunity to read it prior to signing an agreement to purchase any of the lands dealt with in the prospectus.

The act also specifies the information that should be contained in the prospectus for an ordinary subdivision, a strata lot subdivision, and a cooperative corporation or time share plan respectively, and further requires that full, true, and plain disclosure of all the facts relating to the real estate proposed to be sold or leased be made in the prospectus.

It is important to note that the act does not require that the property being sold or leased meet any particular standards, but rather that the standards or particulars of the land be fully disclosed so that it can be determined whether they meet the purchaser's standards.

The real estate prospectus is to protect the prospective purchaser by ensuring that there has been complete and full disclosure of all the facts relevant to the subdivision, such as what services are or are not to be provided, and how the services are being paid for.

The most important sections of the Real Estate Act affecting the general public are sections 59 and 62. Basically, once a prospectus has been accepted by the Superintendent, every purchaser is considered to have relied on the representations made in the prospectus, whether or not that purchaser has, in fact, read the prospectus.

In addition, section 59(1)(b) gives every purchaser of a lot within the subdivision a claim for damages against the promoter for breach of representations made in the prospectus. The purchaser and the promoter are, through these two sections, bound by what the prospectus discloses, regardless of whether or not the purchaser has read it.

Section 62 provides that no agreement to purchase any land covered by Part Two of the Real Estate Act may be enforced against a purchaser of such land by any person who has breached that section.

Thus, if you intend to purchase land to which Part Two of the Real Estate Act applies, you should request a copy of the prospectus. Do not just obtain it — read it and make sure that you thoroughly understand what it contains before agreeing to make your purchase.

If you decide to place an offer on one of the parcels of the property covered by the prospectus, your agent will request that you sign a receipt acknowledging that you have received a copy of the prospectus and that you have been afforded the opportunity to read it. For example, suppose a prospectus states that the purchaser is responsible for installing proper drainage to the land. You will not, once you have signed this receipt, later be able to ask for cancellation of the contract, even if you discover that the property is flooded for six months during the year!

Before leaving the discussion of the Real Estate Act, an interesting point to note is the item under Part One which states that anyone not *licensed* under that part cannot maintain an action for commission in the province for land sold.

With the exception of the subdivision section in chapter 12, it is not within the scope of this book to deal with subdivisions in any further detail except to summarize by saying that anyone owning more than five properties within the same subdivision, whether it was subdivided in 1908 or is just in the process of being subdivided, and who intends to sell or lease such lots, must comply with prospectus requirements of Part Two of the Real Estate Act.

8. Easements and rights-of-way

This discussion applies equally well to both old and new houses. Easements and rights-of-way give certain people special rights regarding a piece of property. When a property is subject to an easement or right-of-way, it will show up on the search of the property.

Easements facilitate the provision of services such as hydro, telephone, water pipes, storm sewers, and sanitary sewers. In order to be of minimum inconvenience to the owner they are usually located along the side or at the rear of the lot lines of the property.

The usual form of easement agreement gives authority to the parties indicated in the agreement to install, maintain, repair, and keep their lines of service in good condition throughout the easement. Most easement agreements also provide that the parties who maintain such services are under an obligation to restore the surface of the property to the same condition as it was prior to the installation or repair.

Also, most easement agreements prohibit the owner of the property from building on top of the easement, whether it be an extensive renovation such as a pool or just a tool shed. If the rights of the owner of a right-of-way agreement or easement are infringed upon, that owner would have a right of action against the person who caused the infringement.

9. New Home Warranty Program

This is a program that has been spearheaded by HUDAC, the Housing and Urban Development Association of Canada. It is a voluntary program subscribed to by certain builders.

The program applies to new homes (single, detached, semi-detached, duplex, townhouse, or a condominium apartment up to four stories) on a permanent foundation built by a registered builder for resale in British Columbia.

Under the terms of the program, it is the builder's responsibility to repair, without charge, defects in materials and/or workmanship according to the terms of the new home warranty certificate and to extend, with all benefits, the remainder of the warranty to subsequent buyers of the certified home during the first year.

During the first year, the program provides protection for the buyer's deposits and down payments to a maximum of $5 000 should the builder become bankrupt or default. It also fulfills the warranty obligations of the builder should he or she default on those. During the second to fifth year inclusive, major structural defects that appear will be repaired (or resolved) up to a maximum of $20 000 over the five-year term of the program.

When a deposit or down payment is received, the builder issues a receipt, which is provided by the program, to the purchaser. This informs the purchaser of the protection afforded under the program. Duplicates of this receipt are immediately forwarded to the New Home Warranty Program office.

Before a new home is occupied, the builder and the purchaser inspect the building and, on a checklist provided by the program, check that the building is complete and note any deficiencies. They both sign the certificate of completion which shows the deficiencies that the builder has agreed to remedy. This certificate is mailed to the program. A warranty certificate is then mailed by the program to the purchaser with a numbered identification sticker to be placed on the electrical breaker boxes as an indication that the house is covered by the program.

If the home owner has a complaint within the first year, he or she notifies the builder. If the parties cannot agree on the work required to be done, either party may submit a written complaint to the program with a fee of $50. The program then appoints an investigator who will, within 14 days, provide both parties with a written decision. If either party is not satisfied with the award, he or she can take other legal remedies. The $50 fee is refundable to the home owner if the home owner is found to be in the right.

There is no charge by the program to the buyer of a home covered by the warranties. Once the builder is registered, the builder pays an insurance fee of $85 per residential unit. A buyer cannot force a builder to join the program so it is likely that only reputable builders who already provide a reasonable warranty will be part of the program.

A list of the registered builders and more information can be obtained from:

> New Home Warranty Program
> of British Columbia
> #760 - 1441 Creekside Drive
> Vancouver, B.C. V6J 4S7
> Telephone: 736-9231

10. Environmental concerns

A new area of concern is the possibility that the land may be contaminated with toxic substances. In the past this has been a "buyer beware" situation, but new cases have found their way around this rule. There are still no uniform rules or approaches to disclosure that vendors must follow. In British

Columbia, the provincial government is introducing legislation to address environmental concerns.

The proposed legislation will establish a registry for properties and a contamination data base. This site registry will become an important source of information for anyone involved in real estate. There will also be guidelines for what is considered contamination and whose responsibility it will be to clean up or remediate the site.

The guidelines also set out different levels of tolerated contamination depending on the proposed use of the property, e.g., commercial or residential. Once the guidelines have been met, a Conditional Certificate of Compliance is issued by the Ministry, which confirms that a remediation plan has been approved and implemented for a contaminated site. Knowing that a remediation plan has been implemented offers some assurance to the purchaser.

If the contamination has migrated to other sites through groundwater, the property owner will also be responsible for remediating these sites. The liability associated with contamination can be very onerous and costly and should not be taken lightly. The person who originally owned the property and contaminated the site will be held responsible, but if that person is not available, the liability falls on the current owner. To avoid this, you must be able to show that you did not cause or contribute to the contamination, and that on purchasing the property, you diligently made inquiries and did not find contamination.

Therefore, you must make inquiries and inspections before you purchase, and the more inspections you make, the better. At the very least, these inquiries should be made through representations and covenants from the vendor. An inquiry can also be done through a Phase 1 Environmental Assessment report. An environmental consulting firm can do this if the cost or concern about the property warrants it. An environmental assessment report is the first step in identifying a contaminated site. The report uses generally available information about the site, such as historical land use from business directories and zoning records, and visual inspection data. Environmental assessment reports are also required by municipal approving officers for any new developments. A report should be available from the developer in a new subdivision.

d. BUYING AN OLDER HOME

1. General

Any of the things that are applicable to buying a new home are also applicable to the purchase of an older home and vice versa. The term "older home" here refers to a home that has been previously occupied, no matter how old it is.

There are certain disadvantages to buying an older home. You could be buying somebody else's problems, such as a leaky roof, pests, or other items that need attention. On the other hand, the landscaping will probably be done and so will that recreation room in the basement, which is usually unfinished in a new home. Similarly, many details such as the screen and shower doors and that extra carpet have probably also been installed. These seemingly little items can add up to a big expense if they have to be done all at one time.

2. Warranties, representations, and inspections

When you are buying an older home, it is obvious that many questions should be asked and satisfactory answers obtained before an offer to purchase is made. What is not obvious is that you can do a great deal to protect yourself by making sure your offer to purchase contains these warranties and representations in writing.

The most important of these could be inserted in the offer as conditions to be met *before* the transaction is closed. An offer to purchase is shown in Sample #3. Please note that it is included only as a sample and is not intended to illustrate the ultimate in protection for a purchaser, for what is important to one purchaser may not be important to another.

SAMPLE #3
INTERIM AGREEMENT (OLDER HOUSE)

INTERIM AGREEMENT
(British Columbia)

THIS OFFER to enter into a binding contract of purchase and sale is made this __22nd__ day

of __January__, 19 _9-_ by __Frederick Flight,__
(insert date)   *(insert names of buyers)*

__Pilot__

(hereinafter called the "Purchaser") having an address of __50 Cessna Crescent,__
(insert civic address)

__Surrey,__   B.C.   A1R 0B1
(municipality)   *(province)*   *(postal code)*   *(telephone number)*

The Purchaser, having inspected the real property described as __747 Boeing Boulevard,__
(civic address)

__Richmond, B.C.__
(municipality)

having a legal description of __Lot "A", Block "B", Section 1, District Lot 123,__
(insert legal description)

__Plan 4567__

(the "Property") on the __22nd__ day of __January__, 19 _9-_ hereby

offers to purchase the Property from the owners thereof (hereinafter called the "Vendor") for the

price and on the terms and subject to the conditions herein set forth, namely:

1. PURCHASE PRICE: The purchase price shall be __Three Hundred and Seventy-five__

__Thousand__ Dollars ($ __375,000.00__) payable as follows:

a.	Paid as a deposit by ☐ *(cash)* ☒ *(cheque)* the sum of:	$	500.00
b.	Cash on completion	$	374,500.00
c.	Balance, if any, as indicated below in the amount of	$	Nil
	TOTAL:	$	375,000.00

Balance, if any, as per paragraph c. above shall be paid as follows:

__All cash on completion__

2. TITLE: The title shall be free and clear of all encumbrances except existing restrictions, exceptions and conditions reserved in favor of the Crown, registered restrictive covenants and rights of way in favor of utilities and public authorities, statutory building schemes, building, zoning and other municipal or governmental restrictions, the existing tenancies specified below, if any, and any other exceptions set out herein. If the Vendor has existing financial encumbrances to clear from the title, the Vendor may wait to pay and discharge such until immediately after receipt of the sales proceeds (provided such is sufficient). In such event, however, the Purchaser shall pay the sales proceeds to a lawyer or notary in trust, on undertakings to pay and discharge the financial encumbrances, and the balance if any, shall be paid to the Vendor.

3. COMPLETION: The sale shall be completed on or before the __28th__ day of __February__, 19 _9-_ (the Completion Date) at the appropriate Land Title Office. Tender or payment of monies by the Purchaser to the Vendor shall be by certified cheque, bank draft, or lawyer's or notary's trust cheque. All documents required to give effect to this contract shall be delivered on or before the Completion Date and shall be, where necessary, in a form acceptable for registration in the appropriate Land Title Office. Time is of the essence and unless the balance of the cash payment is paid and such formal agreement to pay the balance as may be necessary is entered into on or before the Completion Date, the Vendor may, at the Vendor's option, terminate this contract and in such event the amount paid by the Purchaser will be absolutely forfeited to the Vendor on account of damages, without prejudice to the Vendor's other remedies. If the Purchaser is relying upon a new mortgage to finance the purchase of the Property, the Purchaser, while still required to pay the Purchase Price on the Completion Date, may wait to pay the net proceeds of such mortgage to the Purchaser's solicitor until after the transfer and new mortgage documents have been lodged for registration in the appropriate Land Title Office, but only if, before such lodging, the Purchaser has: a) made available for tender to the Vendor that portion of the Purchase Price due on completion less the net proceeds of the new mortgage, and b) fulfilled all the new mortgagee's conditions for funding except lodging of the mortgage for registration, and c) made available to the Vendor a lawyer's or notary's undertaking to pay the balance due on completion upon the lodging of the transfer and new mortgage documents and the advance by the mortgagee of the mortgage proceeds.

SAMPLE #3 — Continued

4. ADJUSTMENTS: The Purchaser will assume and pay all taxes, rates, local improvement assessments, fuel, utilities and other charges from and including the ____1st____ day of ____March____, 19_9-____ (the "Adjustment Date") from which date all adjustments both incoming and outgoing of whatsoever nature will be made and the Vendor shall pay all such charges to such date. The balance of the Purchase Price due on Completion shall reflect such Adjustments.

5. COSTS: The Purchaser will bear all costs of the conveyance, and, if applicable, the costs related to arranging a mortgage and the Vendor will bear all costs of clearing title.

6. POSSESSION: The Purchaser will have vacant possession of the Property at 12:00 noon on the ____1st____ day of ____March____ 19_9- (the "Possession Date") such possession to be a) vacant ☒ or b) subject to the following existing tenancies: N/A

_____

_____

7. RISK: All the buildings on the Property and all other items included in the Purchase Price will be and remain at the risk of the Vendor until 12:01 a.m. on the Completion Date. After that time, the Property and all included items will be at the risk of the Purchaser. In the event that the building or other items included in the purchase and sale are destroyed or substantially damaged prior to Completion, the Purchaser shall elect prior to the Completion Date by notice in writing either to terminate this agreement and have the deposit together with any accrued interest returned or to complete the purchase with the benefit of any insurance proceeds to be for the account of the Purchaser.

8. INCLUDED ITEMS: The Purchase Price includes any buildings, improvements, fixtures, appurtenances and attachments thereto and all blinds, awnings, screen doors and windows, curtain rods, tracks and valences, fixed mirrors, fixed carpeting, electric, plumbing, heating and air conditioning fixtures and all appurtenances and attachments thereto as viewed by the Purchaser at the date of inspection including

    all as per builder's specifications attached _____

_____

_____

_____

but excluding ____Nil_____

_____

_____

The Property and all included items shall be in substantially the same condition at the Possession Date as when viewed by the Purchaser on the Inspection date.

9. CONDITIONS: In addition to all other conditions contained herein, the Purchaser is submitting this offer on the following express conditions, which conditions the Vendor by accepting this offer warrants and represents to be true, namely:

    a. The Property has been used only as a residential property by the Vendor until the date of sale and is exempt from the payment of GST on sale;

    b. The Vendor is not now nor will 60 days after the Possession Date be a non-resident of Canada within the meaning of the Income Tax Act of Canada nor is the Vendor the agent or trustee for anyone with an interest in this property who is or will, 60 days from the Possession Date, be a non-resident of Canada within the meaning of the Income Tax Act of Canada.

    c. The attached Property Condition Disclosure Statement dated the ____22nd____ day of ____January____, 19_9- is true and correct and is incorporated into this contract and forms an integral part thereof.

    d. The Property has ☐ has not ☒ been insulated with urea formaldehyde.

    e. Other ____see Schedule "A" attached hereto which forms____

           part of this Interim Agreement._____

_____

f. Each condition contained in this agreement is for the sole benefit of the party indicated, where so indicated and unless each condition is waived or declared fulfilled by written notice given by the benefiting party to the other party on or before the date specified for each condition, this contract will thereupon be terminated and any deposit paid hereunder shall be immediately returned.

10. GENERAL:

a. There are no warranties, representations, guarantees, promises, or agreements other than those set out herein, all of which shall survive the completion of the sale.

b. Any reference to a party in this contract includes that party's heirs, executors, administrators, and assigns and the singular includes the plural and the feminine includes the masculine.

11. TIME FOR ACCEPTANCE: This offer (or counter-offer as the case may be) is open for acceptance until __5:00__ o'clock __P__ m on the __5th__ day of __January__ 19 __9-__

and upon acceptance thereof in writing with notification to the other party of such acceptance.

THIS CONTRACT SHALL BE A BINDING CONTRACT OF PURCHASE AND SALE ON THE TERMS AND CONDITIONS SET OUT HEREIN.

Freddy Flight	Frederick Flight	
Purchaser	Print name	Witness

Purchaser	Print name	Witness

THE VENDOR HEREBY ACCEPTS THE ABOVE OFFER THIS _____ 24th _____ DAY OF

_____ January _____, 19 _9-_, acknowledges receipt of the deposit, and agrees to complete the sale on the terms and conditions set out herein.
ACE BUILDERS INC.
Per: _Jack O'Altrades_

Vendor	Print name	Witness

Vendor	Print name	Witness

#5,555 No. 5 Road, Richmond, B.C.
Vendor's address

	273-0001
Home phone	Work phone

CONVEYANCING INFORMATION:

Rich Slickenfast	246-8010
Name of purchaser's lawyer/notary	Phone

999 Golden Brick Lane, Vancouver, B.C.
Address

Hope Riches	649-1000
Name of vendor's lawyer/notary	Phone

1001 Lotto Lane, Vancouver, B.C.
Address

SCHEDULE "A"

To the Interim Agreement dated January 22, 199- where Frederick Flight is Purchaser of the property know as 747 Boeing Boulevard, Richmond, B.C.

1.   This transaction is subject to the Purchaser arranging a new First Mortgage within fourteen (14) business days of the date of this offer in the minimum amount of $165,000 with interest thereon not to exceed 8 1/2% per annum, calculated half yearly, not in advance, having a minimum five (5) year amortization. Such subject shall be deemed to have been waived unless the Purchaser specifically informs the Vendor otherwise in writing within fourteen (14) business days of the date of this offer.

PROVIDED FURTHER that the Vendor's rights to accept further offers for the property described herein are hereby reserved provided that in the event another acceptable offer is received, the Purchaser is to be given written notice thereof and 24 hours in which to remove the subject clause failing which the Vendor shall be free to accept such new offer.

2.   The following are conditions for the completion of the within transaction by the Purchaser, which conditions are for the benefit of the Purchaser only and may be waived by him in writing at any time hereafter:

(a)   That the dwelling on the real property will be constructed in accordance with and will as of closing, comply with all relevant municipal, provincial, and federal requirements;

(b)   That there are no easements, rights-of-way or encroachments of any kind whatsoever affecting the real property, save and except for an easement in favour of the City of Richmond, which easement is located along the rear six feet of the said property.

3.   It is understood and agreed as follows:

(a)   That in the event completion of the dwelling on the real property is delayed for any reason whatsoever, the Vendor shall be permitted an extension of the time for closing of up to sixty (60) days and the time of closing shall be extended accordingly. If at the time of such extended period, the Vendor shall have been unable to complete the building on the real property, this Agreement shall be terminated at the option of the Purchaser, and the deposit shall be returned to the Purchaser without interest or

2

deduction whatsoever and the Vendor shall not be liable to the Purchaser for any damages whatsoever. It is understood and agreed that the dwelling on the real property shall be conclusively deemed to have been completed if all the interior work, save for minor items of construction, shall be completed;

(b)   The Purchaser shall be entitled to withhold 10% of the value of the improvements for forty-one (41) days pursuant to the provisions of the Builders Lien Act provided that the amount of such lien holdback is held in trust by the Purchaser's solicitor or the solicitor for the Purchaser's mortgage company in an interest bearing trust account for such lien holdback period and that the same, together with accumulated interest thereon less any amounts required to discharge any liens that may be filed during such period, be paid to the Vendor at the expiration of such lien holdback period without further deduction.

4.   The Vendor covenants and agrees as follows:

(a)   To complete construction of the dwelling on the real property in accordance with the plans and specifications shown to the Purchaser and initialled by him in accordance with the provisions of the builder's specifications attached hereto. The Vendor shall have the right to substitute other material provided for in these plans and specifications subject to the approval of the Purchaser.

If you are not sure what you are doing, it is far better for you to spend a small amount at this point in obtaining expert advice from a lawyer or someone else familiar with the real estate business than a large amount later trying to get out of a bad deal.

This technique of reducing the important representations to writing in the offer is an excellent way of flushing out potential problems. If, for example, the vendor is asked to make certain warranties and representations in the interim agreement and signs it as having accepted it, that vendor is then legally committed. If, however, the vendor crosses out an item in the offer, you are being alerted to a potential problem and you can then pursue the matter and make further inquiries.

It goes without saying that you should carefully inspect the home before submitting an offer. As a matter of fact, it is a good idea to inspect the home a minimum of three times, preferably once on a sunny day, once on a rainy day, and once at night.

Visual inspection of the house will reveal water stains, the condition of the painting, plastering, carpets, lights and light fixtures, etc. It will not reveal, however, whether certain other items require repair — such as the roof, furnace, hot water tank, or the condition of the electrical, plumbing, and heating systems. Also worth close inspection in these days of high energy costs is the amount and quality of insulation. Problems with any of these could be very costly.

In some areas commercial house inspection services exist. For approximately $150, an experienced person will inspect the house thoroughly. To determine what the insulation situation is, you can use an infra-red scan available through independent inspectors or insulation companies. The cost is about $80. Considering the cost of the house, the price of an inspection is well worth it. If there is no commercial inspection service in your area, it is highly recommended that you contact someone knowledgeable in home construction and pay that person to look the house over thoroughly and have the place inspected for pests. Remember that it may be too late to do anything about serious problems discovered after you have moved in. You *must* protect yourself beforehand.

In short, *inspect, ask questions, obtain satisfactory answers*, and *insert warranties* into the offer. Failure to take these steps could result in your being forced to complete the transaction for a home full of deficiencies or forfeiting the deposit for failing to complete the transaction, and/or being sued for damages for being in breach of contract.

The B.C. Real Estate Association has recognized the existence of some of these problems and has devised a residential disclosure statement. This is a simple form containing a series of basic questions about the house that vendors answer to the best of their ability and sign. The completion of such a statement is voluntary. However, should a seller refuse to make the disclosure, let it be a warning to the purchaser. These disclosure statements have now become a standard tool for many real estate agents, who have often gotten caught between a vendor and an unhappy purchaser. By having a properly completed disclosure statement signed by the vendor and given to the purchaser, there is a record of what has been disclosed. Any purchaser would, therefore, have difficulty claiming either misrepresentation or that important information was withheld. Not only does the purchaser have the information, but the vendor is assured all the information is passed on to the purchaser. The realtor is also protected since there now exists a written record of what the vendor has represented and what the realtor can pass on to the purchaser.

The disclosure statement and the representations in it can be made part of the interim agreement by including the following as a clause in the interim agreement:

> The attached Property Condition Disclosure Statement dated _____ is incorporated into this contract and forms an integral part thereof.

This, however, does not replace the old maxim "Buyer Beware." Even though a disclosure statement has been given or made part of the contract, prudent purchasers should still make their own enquiries. Even a successful lawsuit is extremely expensive and will not guarantee that damages can be recovered from an insolvent vendor. It is, therefore, strongly recommended that a house inspection be carried out and that the cost of repairing any problems be established before purchase. Sample #4 shows the Property Condition Disclosure Statement developed by the B.C. Real Estate Association.

3. Rights-of-way and easements

As with new homes, you should also ask about any existing encroachments, rights-of-way, and easements. These could be of very special importance to the purchaser, if for instance, the lot that you are buying has a hydro easement running right through the middle making it impossible to build a house. Therefore, watch out. Most standard interim agreements used in British Columbia require the vendor to deliver clear title except as disclosed in the agreement. Most agreements provide for clear title except when there are "restrictive covenants, existing tenancies, reservations and exceptions in the original grant from the Crown, easements in favor of utilities and public authority." (See also chapter 4.)

Normally a purchaser is willing to accept title, subject to easements, rights-of-way, or encroachments, but you, as purchaser, should at least be aware of them and know what they are. You should also attempt to obtain a survey certificate from the vendor. A survey certificate is the drawing of a property showing the location of dwellings on the property, the boundaries of the property, and any easement, rights-of-way, or encroachments that affect the title to the property as

SAMPLE #4
PROPERTY CONDITION DISCLOSURE STATEMENT*

PROPERTY CONDITION DISCLOSURE STATEMENT

Date of disclosure: _____

The following is a statement made by the sellers concerning the condition of the property or strata unit located at:

ADDRESS/(STRATA UNIT #):

THE SELLERS ARE RESPONSIBLE FOR THE ACCURACY OF THE ANSWERS ON THIS DISCLOSURE STATEMENT AND WHERE UNCERTAIN SHOULD REPLY "DO NOT KNOW". THIS DISCLOSURE STATEMENT WILL FORM PART OF THE CONTRACT OF PURCHASE AND SALE IF SO AGREED IN WRITING BY THE SELLERS AND BUYERS.

THE SELLERS SHOULD INITIAL THE APPROPRIATE REPLIES

1. GENERAL:	YES	NO	DO NOT KNOW	DOES NOT APPLY
A. Are the premises connected to public sewer system?				
B. Are the premises connected to public water system?				
C. Are the premises connected to a private or a community water system?				
D. Are you aware of any problems re: quantity or quality of well water? (Gal. per minute if known: _____)				
E. Are you aware of any problems with the septic system? (Date of last service: _____)				
F. Do the premises contain unauthorized accommodation?				
G. Are you aware of any encroachments, unregistered easements or unregistered rights of way?				
H. Are you aware of, or have you been charged any local improvement levies/charges?				
I. Have you received any other notice or claim affecting the property from any person or public body?				

2. STRUCTURAL:	YES	NO	DO NOT KNOW	DOES NOT APPLY
A. To the best of your knowledge, are the exterior walls insulated?				
B. To the best of your knowledge, is the ceiling insulated?				
C. To the best of your knowledge, have the premises ever contained asbestos insulation?				
D. To the best of your knowledge, have the premises ever contained urea formaldahyde insulation?				
E. Has a final building inspection been approved or an unconditional occupancy permit been obtained?				
F. Has the wood stove/fireplace insert installation been approved by local authorities?				
G. Are you aware of any additions or alterations made without a required permit?				
H. Are you aware of any structural problems with the premises or other buildings on the property?				
I. Are you aware of any problems with the heating and/or central air conditioning system?				
J. Are you aware of any moisture and/or water problems in the basement or crawl space?				
K. Are you aware of any damage due to wind, fire, water?				
L. Are you aware of any infestation by insects or rodents?				
M. Are you aware of any roof leakage or unrepaired damage? (Age of roof if known: _____ years)				
N. Are you aware of any problems with the electrical system?				
O. Are you aware of any problems with the plumbing system?				
P. Are you aware of any problems with the swimming pool and/or hot tub?				

3. STRATA UNIT:	YES	NO	DO NOT KNOW	DOES NOT APPLY
A. Are you aware of any special assessments voted on or proposed?				
B. Are you aware of any pending strata council policy or by-law amendments which may alter the uses of the unit?				
C. Are there any restrictions on pets, children or rentals?				

4. ADDITIONAL COMMENTS AND/OR EXPLANATIONS: (Use additional pages if necessary)

_____

_____

_____

_____

The sellers state that the above information is true, based on the sellers' current actual knowledge as of the above date. Any important changes to this information made known to the sellers will be disclosed by sellers to buyers prior to closing. The sellers acknowledge receipt of a copy of this disclosure statement and agree that a copy may be given to prospective buyers.

PLEASE READ INFORMATION ON THE REVERSE SIDE OF THIS FORM

SELLER _____ SELLER _____

The buyers acknowledge that they have received and read a signed copy of this disclosure statement from the sellers or the sellers' agent on the _____ day of _____, 199___. The prudent buyers will use this disclosure statement as the starting point for their own inquiries.

The buyers are urged to carefully inspect the property and, if desired, to have the property inspected by an inspection service of their choice.

BUYER _____ BUYER _____

Sellers and buyers understand that neither the listing nor selling agencies or their representatives warrant or guarantee the above information on the property.

THIS FORM IS PRINTED ON 50% RECYCLED PAPER USING VEGETABLE OIL BASED INKS.

*Reproduced with the kind permission of the B.C. Real Estate Association.

of a certain date. A proper survey certificate in British Columbia is prepared by a B.C. land surveyor and costs about $120.

There is one way to save this expense — as outlined in the next section.

4. Survey certificates

A survey certificate is an important document in the purchase of a home for several reasons.

First, it allows you to see where the foundations of the house are located relative to the property lines.

It also allows you to determine whether the fences are located in the right place. If they are located inside the boundaries of the property being purchased, you are, in actual fact, purchasing more property than is at first indicated. If they are located outside the property being purchased, you could be buying a future lawsuit by one of the neighbors for using property that is not yours or having to remove them at your expense.

Third, a survey certificate will show whether the property being purchased is encroaching on or being encroached upon by neighboring lands. An encroachment is the use of one's property in such a way that it interferes with the use of another person's property in any way. An example of this would be if the garage on the land being purchased was located slightly on the neighbor's property. Such a situation could be the makings of a lawsuit. If discovered beforehand, however, it can be easily remedied by either removing the item that is encroaching, if that is feasible, or by obtaining an agreement in writing signed by the neighbor, permitting the encroachment.

The fourth reason for obtaining a survey certificate is to discover the existence and to determine the location of easements and rights-of-way that may exist over the property. This becomes especially important if there has been any construction done on an easement or right-of-way, as the person who has the benefit of the use of such easement or right-of-way (e.g., B.C. Hydro) may have the legal right to have it removed at your expense.

The fifth and probably most immediate reason for obtaining a survey certificate is that the mortgage company may very well require one before advancing the mortgage money. You may be able to save some money if the vendor has an old certificate lying about. If not, and if there is an outstanding mortgage on the place, contact the mortgage company involved, as it may have one on file and you could obtain a copy.

It is, of course, essential that no additions or alterations have been made to the home that may affect the distances to the lot boundaries since the survey was done.

5. What about the appliances and other chattels?

In addition to the sale of the real estate, the vendor, on many occasions, wants to dispose of other items, such as the washer and dryer, stove and fridge, drapes, and built-in dishwasher. The general rule is that if they are permanently attached to the land or building they automatically form part of the real property unless they are specifically excluded. These items include built-in dishwashers, built-in wall ovens, attached light fixtures, and attached mirrors.

If they are movable, they are not part of the property; for instance, curtains (as opposed to drapery tracks that are usually permanently attached), fridges, and stoves. In order to avoid any dispute as to whether a specific item is part of the property or not, you should list in full detail all the items that are included in the offer. Note also that there will be sales tax payable on any "movables" that the vendor sells. (See chapter 4.)

6. Revenue suites

Some homes also contain revenue suites. The appropriate zoning bylaws for the area could have the effect of making such a revenue suite illegal and the municipality could theoretically force you to discontinue renting the suite or suites with a consequent loss of revenue. If the prospective purchaser is counting on such revenue, this could be a great loss and, in this case, you should make legality of the tenancy a condition of the completion of the transaction.

During a housing shortage, the practice of most municipalities is to "look the other way" at illegal suites unless a nuisance is created or formal complaint lodged. As a purchaser, the extra revenue may be attractive to you, but perhaps the status of the suite would lower the price somewhat. It is always a question of negotiation.

Where there is a tenant, you should, in addition, find out the terms of the tenancy — whether it is written or verbal, the term of the lease or tenancy, the rental amount, the date of the last rental increase, and whether or not the tenant has any further right to renew the tenancy.

This information should be obtained prior to submitting the offer. In addition, the interim agreement should provide, as a condition for closing, that the owner obtain written confirmation from the tenant of the terms and conditions of that tenancy.

Also, if you want vacant possession (i.e., the tenant out) make that a condition of closing. In this way it is the vendor's problem to deal with the tenant. Otherwise it becomes yours.

7. Are you purchasing property from a non-resident?

Section 116 of the Income Tax Act deals with the purchase of property from people who are not residents of Canada within the meaning of the Income Tax Act.

A person who is not a resident of Canada is subject to a tax of 25% on capital gains obtained in Canada. The problem of imposing a tax on non-residents of Canada is the collection of the tax and section 116 of the act attempts to enforce collection of the tax from the vendor by putting a very large responsibility on the purchaser of the property.

Under this section, a vendor who is not a resident of Canada must apply to the government of Canada for a certificate which, when issued, will assess the vendor's tax liability for the property. Thus, if the purchaser pays a greater price than that set forth in the certificate, the purchaser may be responsible for tax on the difference between the price paid and the certificate limit.

The Income Tax Act further imposes a responsibility on the purchaser to make reasonable inquiries to determine the country of residence of the vendor. If the purchaser fails to make these inquiries or the vendor does not provide a satisfactory answer to these inquiries, the act provides that the *purchaser* will be responsible for the payment of the 25% tax.

Where a non-resident vendor does not apply for a certificate and the purchaser nevertheless wishes to complete the transaction, the purchaser is required to withhold 15% of the entire purchase price. This can then be released to the vendor when he or she obtains the certificate.

Thus, it is common in current real estate transactions for the purchaser to require from the vendor either the certificate described in section 116 of the act or evidence in the form of a sworn statement or otherwise from the vendor that the vendor is a resident of Canada within the meaning of section 116.

What happens if the vendor is unwilling to apply for the necessary certificate or if the vendor is unwilling to provide satisfactory evidence of residency in Canada and the purchaser chooses to sign the agreement anyway?

It creates a real dilemma, since it is felt that the provisions of section 116 of the act do not amount to a lien against the real estate but remain as personal obligations between the parties.

Thus, if the vendor should fail to comply with the responsibilities under section 116, the purchaser cannot refuse to complete the transaction on the basis that the vendor is not conveying a good title. Moreover, by refusing to close, the purchaser may be liable to the vendor for the loss of the deposit, specific performance, or damages.

On the other hand, by completing the transaction, the purchaser may be liable to the government of Canada for the 15% of the purchase price that should have been withheld.

This problem can be avoided if the purchaser places an obligation on the vendor in the interim agreement to comply with section 116 either by obtaining the necessary certificate or, alternatively, by providing satisfactory evidence of residency in Canada — failing which, the purchaser shall have the right to withhold 15% of the sale price until such requirements are satisfied.

It is important to keep in mind that the term "residency" has a specific meaning for the purposes of the Income Tax Act. This term also applies to corporations, associations of people, and trusts and, thus, the purchase of real estate from a company, a firm, or an estate does not relieve the purchaser of obligations under this section.

4

THE INTERIM AGREEMENT OR OFFER TO PURCHASE

a. WHAT IS AN INTERIM AGREEMENT?

Samples #2 and #3, which are shown in the previous chapter, are two examples of interim agreements. Sample #2 is for the purchase of a new house and Sample #3 is for the purchase of an older house. As mentioned previously, these forms are inserted only as examples of interim agreements and are not meant to represent the perfect answer for everyone. Other forms are also used.

The interim agreement or offer to purchase is exactly that — an offer to purchase by the purchaser which, on the acceptance by the vendor, becomes a legally binding contract (providing it meets all the requirements of a contract — as previously discussed). Once accepted, it is, in fact, an interim agreement until either the transaction is closed and the final documents are signed, or the interim agreement lapses. Again, it must be reiterated that *it is one of the most important documents that you will ever sign in your lifetime.*

Although the interim agreement is, in most circumstances, an unimposing pre-printed form, great care should still be taken to see that it outlines the transaction accurately. Once the contract is in writing it is not possible to later add to it in court a verbal explanation of what was meant, understood, or intended.

Many people believe that a printed contract cannot be altered. That is not so. The printing is only for the convenience of the user. If you do not agree with something in the printed contract, alter it, delete it, or amend it, *but do not ignore it!* If changes are made on the form, all parties should sign their initials to the change.

In most instances, the real estate agent writes up the interim agreement on behalf of the purchaser, and submits it to the vendor for consideration. The real estate agent, who may in some instances also be the vendor's agent, will then present the offer to the vendor and attempt to get him or her to accept the offer. The vendor may do one of the following:

(a) Reject the offer outright by refusing to sign it

OR

(b) Accept the offer by signing it in the form that it is presented without alteration

OR

(c) Counter-offer, that is, vary some term in the interim agreement and send it back to the prospective purchaser for approval. Remember that a counter-offer is, in essence, a rejection of the initial offer followed by an offer to sell. Once the vendor counter-offers, the purchaser is no longer bound by the first offer and the vendor cannot later decide to accept it, thus binding the purchaser.

Let us now deal with some of the standard items in an interim agreement.

b. CONTENTS OF AN INTERIM AGREEMENT

1. The deposit (What you lose if you don't complete)

The deposit serves two purposes.

(a) It is part payment of the purchase price which is the consideration for the sale and is, thus, one of the legal requirements for a contract.

(b) It is a guarantee of performance.

When a real estate agent is involved in the sale, the deposit is usually paid to the agent's company and held in trust by it, pending completion of the transaction. After the transaction has been completed, it is turned over to the vendor. However, since the vendor in most instances owes the real estate agent commission, the deposit is retained by the agent and applied against the commission. If it is the purchaser's fault that the purchase is not completed, the vendor is entitled to keep the deposit.

However, if the transaction is handled through a real estate agent, the interim agreement usually specifies that, in such a case, the deposit must be paid to the agent by the vendor to compensate for that agent's effort. A pre-printed interim agreement can be changed to allow the vendor a share of any forfeited deposit to help compensate for any damages incurred.

If the transaction fails to close due to the fault of the vendor or if there is no contract at all, the deposit should be returned to the purchaser. If the purchaser and vendor cannot agree on what is to happen to the commission, the agent may pay the money into court and let the court settle the issue.

2. Subject offers (How to get out of a deal)

When there is a condition precedent ("subject to" clause) in the interim agreement, it means that there is not a firm contract for purchase and sale until that condition has been fulfilled *or* been waived by the party for whose benefit it was inserted.

For instance, if our friends Hilda and Harry Homeseeker wish to make an offer to purchase a house but know that they will require a new mortgage, their offer could include the following clause to protect them if, for some reason, they are not able to arrange the mortgage:

> This offer is subject to the purchasers arranging a conventional first mortgage within fourteen (14)

business days of the date of this offer in the amount of $100 000 with interest at not more than 10 1/4% per annum calculated semi-annually and a 25-year amortization.

Such a "subject to" clause is inserted in order not only to protect their right to have their deposit returned if they are unsuccessful in finding a mortgage, but also to protect them against a possible lawsuit for completion of a contract that was, to them, still uncertain.

The terms of the mortgage that Harry and Hilda want to find should be specified or the offer could be void due to uncertainty with the result that the vendor could pull out at any time. If Harry and Hilda do not want to limit their options to get out of the contract, they can leave the terms wide open but would run the risk that the vendor could elect to treat the interim agreement as void. On the other hand, if the vendor does not want to give Harry and Hilda an easy way to get out of the agreement, the vendor should make the "subject to" clause as specific as possible.

Other examples of "subject to" clauses that provide the purchasers with an "out" are:

> This offer to purchase is subject to the purchasers selling their home at 007 Bond Avenue, Action City, for a minimum of $75 000 cash with a completion prior to the completion date set out herein.

(This clause should be inserted where the purchasers do not want to buy a new house before they know that the old one is sold. They can then use the money from the sale of their house in completing their new purchase.)

OR

> This offer to purchase is subject to approval as to form and contents by the purchasers' solicitor, I. Knowitall. Such approval is to be communicated to the vendors within five (5) days of acceptance or be deemed to be withheld.

This clause can be used not only as an "out," but also for the purchasers' protection when they genuinely wish to obtain their lawyer's opinion and advice.

Every "subject to" clause should contain a date or time by which the subject is either removed or the offer lapses. With such a clause in the interim agreement, the parties must realize that the deal may never be completed. The vendor, however, is obligated to sell if the condition is met or waived by the purchaser, if it is a condition in favor of the purchaser. The vendor can also insert "subject to" clauses into the interim agreement which, if they are met or waived, would obligate the purchaser to purchase or be liable for damages.

If the purchaser presents a "subject to" offer to the vendor, the vendor could, to leave the options open, insert the following clause:

> The vendor reserves the right to accept further offers for the property described herein, provided that in the event another acceptable offer is received, Mr. and Mrs. Homeseeker are to be given written notice thereof and 24 hours in which to remove all subjects, failing which the vendor shall be free to accept the new offer.

When a subject has been satisfied, it should be removed. This is done in an acknowledgment signed by both parties stating, for instance:

> That certain subject clause contained in the Interim Agreement dated January 2, 199- between Hilda and Harry Homeseeker as "purchasers" and Peter Sellers as "vendor" reading:
>
> > "This offer is subject to the purchasers' arranging a first mortgage within 14 business days of the date of this offer in the amount of $100 000 on terms satisfactory to them."
>
> is hereby removed, making the Interim Agreement a firm and binding agreement of purchase and sale.

The reason both parties sign the "subject removal" is that some "subjects" could be construed to be for the benefit of both the vendor and purchaser. By having both parties agree to remove the subject, the potentially contentious issue is removed if the vendor, for example, subsequently wished to get out of the agreement.

If the purchaser truly wants the subject to be for his or her benefit only, the following should be inserted after the subject to clause.

> This subject is for the purchaser's benefit only and may be waived in writing, in whole or in part, unilaterally by the purchaser.

This allows the purchaser to remove the subject without having to worry about obtaining the approval or concurrence of the vendor.

3. Adjustment date (After this the purchaser pays)

The interim agreement should provide for a date from which the purchaser will assume the payment of all taxes, water rates, electricity, heat, rentals, and all other adjustments that are to be made between the parties. It is from that date that all benefits and obligations are assumed by the purchaser.

An example would be the payment of taxes. Although some municipalities have now altered their tax year to provide for payment of property taxes twice a year, property taxes are still commonly paid once a year. The tax year usually runs from January 1 to December 31, and the taxes are usually payable halfway through that year, say July 1. If the adjustment date is, for example, April 1, that means the taxes for the year have not been paid yet.

Thus, the purchaser who will be living in the house on July 1, will have to pay the taxes for the whole year including the months prior to March 31 when the vendor was still living in the house. The purchaser is, therefore, entitled to be reimbursed by the vendor for the first three months. That is, if the taxes are $1 200 per year, the vendor would owe the purchaser $1 200 x 3⁄12, or $300. Similarly, if the adjustment date is November 1 and the vendor has already paid the year's taxes, the purchaser will have to reimburse the vendor for the months of November and December.

If the adjustment date is before the taxes for the year have been finalized, it is customary to adjust the taxes on the basis of last year's taxes with a provision for a reasonable increase. The parties usually agree to make any further adjustments between themselves when the final tax figures become available. Similarly, it is customary to adjust on the net amount of the taxes. In other words, where the taxes for the year are $1 200 but the person who will be or has paid the taxes during the year is entitled to a home-owner's grant of, say, $380, the taxes should be adjusted to be based on $820 for that year.

Where a mortgage is being assumed by the purchaser, the adjustment can also sometimes create difficulties. Suppose the adjustment date is April 1 and the payment under the mortgage that is being assumed is also due on that date. In this case, the purchaser should make the payment. But if the adjustment date is April 2, the payment is the vendor's responsibility. This does not save the purchaser any money, however, as the following example illustrates:

Balance due on the mortgage as of March 1	$10 000
Interest from March 1 up to and including April 1	100
Balance due under mortgage as of April 1	$10 100
April 1 mortgage payment	125
Balance due under the mortgage after April 1 payment	$9 975

Assume the purchase price is $20 000, with no other adjustments. If the purchaser makes the mortgage payment, the purchaser's payment to the vendor is:

Purchase price	$20 000
Less mortgage assumed on April 1	10 100
Payment to vendor	$9 900

In addition, the purchaser makes the mortgage payments of $125, for a total payment of $10 025.

If the adjustment date is April 2, the vendor makes the mortgage payment and the purchaser owes the vendor $10 025, this amount being the same total owed as the previous example indicated and calculated as follows:

Purchase price	$20 000
Balance due under the mortgage being assumed after April 1 payment	9 975
Total amount payable to vendor	$10 025

The above examples show that the money payable by the purchaser is the same in both instances. Actually, if the adjustment date is April 2, the purchaser will be credited with one day's interest for the day of April 1 for which the vendor would be responsible, but this is, in most instances, a relatively minor amount. Most adjustments are set out in the Statement of Adjustments prepared by the purchaser's lawyer. This document is discussed further in section **d.** in chapter 9.

Although the adjustment date is a matter of contract or agreement between the parties and can theoretically be any date, the most common date to use is the date of possession.

77

4. Possession date (Home sweet home)

This is the date on which the vendor has contracted to give the purchaser possession of the house. Since the purchaser can start using the house on that date, it is only fair that the purchaser should assume the expenses from that date, and that is usually the reason that the adjustment dates and the possession dates are the same. This is by no means a requirement, as it is a matter of contract left entirely to the parties, but in most instances, it makes the most sense.

If you are a vendor, the possession date should preferably be a couple of days after the completion date (see next section) or even on the same date, but *never* before the completion date. This would allow the completion to take place and the money to exchange hands before the purchaser is allowed possession. If the purchaser is allowed possession prior to completion, there is less incentive to complete the little details that have to be attended to before completion which could, thus, be inconveniently delayed. Furthermore, if the purchaser suddenly, for some reason, is unable to complete, the vendor is faced with having to evict someone who could be quite reluctant to give up possession. And it is not an easy matter to evict someone in these circumstances.

5. Completion date (Money changes hands)

This is a crucial date — the date when all the documentation must be signed, sealed, and delivered — and the money paid. Most interim agreements contain a little phrase "time is of the essence in this agreement." This means that both the vendor and the purchaser have the right to insist on completion on the scheduled date, failing which they may, at their option, cancel the agreement. This is a complicated area of the law and professional guidance should be sought immediately at the first sign of any problems. Nevertheless, if you are anxious that the transaction not be jeopardized, you should make doubly sure that you have done everything required by the closing date. If this is not possible, an extension of the closing date, in writing, should be obtained.

Normally, in real estate transactions in British Columbia, the purchaser has the responsibility of preparing all the conveyancing documentation and paying all the costs of the conveyancing. The vendor, after contracting to provide clear title, is responsible for clearing the title and looking after all costs in connection with that.

On the completion date, the conveyancing documents that are registered in the Land Title Office are filed there, and after the title has been checked (to make sure that the purchaser has received satisfactory title), the purchase money is paid. This is, in most instances, handled by the purchaser's lawyer and the procedure is discussed in more detail in chapter 9.

6. Insurance and risk (Who insures)

The interim agreement should also specify at what point the risk passes from the vendor to the purchaser. Some interim agreements provide that the property is at the risk of the purchaser from the time of acceptance of the offer while the majority of interim agreements currently in use provide that the property is at the risk of the vendor until the time of delivery of the conveyance or the completion date. This is preferable.

In this situation it is recommended that the purchaser insure from the time of (and including) the completion date, while the vendor should wait until after the completion date before terminating insurance. If the risk has passed to the purchaser as of the date of acceptance of the offer, the purchaser should insure the property as of that date in order to protect the investment.

7. Fixtures and movable property (What is included)

As previously mentioned, items that are movable are usually classified as chattels; items that are not movable are considered fixtures. Fixtures without specific mention are automatically included in the sale price. Chattels are not.

Thus, fridges, stoves, dishwashers, curtains, and loose laid carpet are classified as chattels, whereas built-in fridges, stoves, dishwashers, curtain rods, and attached wall-to-wall carpet are considered fixtures.

Should you as purchaser wish to include chattels in the purchase, and for that matter in the purchase price, these items should specifically be mentioned in the interim agreement as being included. They should also be specifically identified so the vendor will not, for instance, take out the nice expensive curtains you like and replace them with some older, garish, less expensive curtains that may be totally unacceptable to you. This would be defensible if the interim agreement had said:

> Vendor to supply curtains for all windows, cost of
> which shall be included in the purchase price.

Suddenly, you have another hefty bill you were not counting on, and, believe me, it happens.

The Social Service Tax Act of our province should also be kept in mind. It provides that a sales tax be paid for any chattel (movable property) purchased when buying a house. The current sales tax is 6% of the value of the chattel. Where no value is allocated to the chattel, the tax is 6% of the market value.

The tax must be paid either to the vendor, who is then obligated to forward it to the government, or to the government directly. There is no sales tax on fixtures. Technically, insofar as the sales tax is concerned, it does not matter whether the purchase price of the house is a set price that includes the chattels, or whether extra is paid for the chattels.

If a single price has been negotiated, including the chattels, the interim agreement should specify a fair value for the chattels, upon which both parties have agreed. The sales tax should then be calculated on this price.

There may be a problem deciding what is a fixture and what is not. Obviously, from the purchaser's point of view, the more objects classified as fixtures, the better, and, as long as the items are properly accounted for, there should be no objection on the part of the vendor to this classification. However, it is not wise to carry this policy too far, as some items, such as chairs, are obviously movable items and require the sales tax which, if not paid, could cause an assessment to be issued by the provincial tax department, together with penalties.

However, as the tax is based on the fair market value of the chattels and as it is very difficult to evaluate used furniture or appliances, the tax can be mitigated by allocating most of the purchase price to the property and only a small amount to the chattels.

8. Commissions (So that's why the agent was so nice)

When a vendor has listed a property with a real estate agent, it is the real estate agent's job to find a purchaser for that property. For this service, the real estate agent is paid a commission, which is, in most instances, based on a percentage of the sale price.

If the property has been put on multiple listing, the standard commission rate is currently 7% of the sale price. The commission on a standard exclusive listing for a residential property is currently 5%, while vacant land is usually more, although usually negotiable. For properties having a value in excess of $100 000, the standard commission is 5% for an exclusive listing and 7% for a multiple listing on the first $100 000 and 2½% on the balance thereafter.

The agreement to pay commission is set out in the listing agreement. However, on the bottom of most interim agreements, there is also a section setting out the commission charged, which the vendor confirms when accepting an offer.

This section usually also provides that if the sale is not completed due to a fault of the purchaser, the real estate agent is entitled to keep the deposit as compensation. If you don't agree with this policy, change it. There is no magic in a printed form that prevents it from being changed.

As previously discussed, the real estate agent will generally ask the prospective purchaser to pay a deposit, which is then held by the agent's company in a trust account. This deposit is the first source of commission payable to the real estate agent or salesperson.

When a binding interim agreement has been made, it is standard practice for a real estate company to send a sales report to the vendor's and purchaser's lawyers. This sales report will list the details of the transaction, including the deposit held and the total commission payable. The company will also request the purchaser's lawyer to deduct the deposit from the commission owed and forward the balance directly to the real estate company on completion. Such payment is usually authorized by the vendor when signing the Statement of Adjustments (to be discussed later) so the purchaser's lawyer thus has authority to comply with the request of the real estate company.

Once the commission is received by the real estate company, it is split between the listing salesperson, the selling salesperson, their companies, and where applicable, the multiple listing service.

9. The fine print

The body of a standard interim agreement contains a fair amount of fine print which you must pay attention to. Some of the items have already been discussed in the previous sections, some have not.

The covenant of the vendor that the property be "free and clear of other encumbrances except restrictive covenants, existing tenancies, reservations and exceptions in the original grant from the Crown, easements in favor of utilities and public authorities and except as set out above" is a very important covenant, the contents of which should be thoroughly explored. This covenant expressly permits:

(a) Restrictive covenants: this is an agreement the purchaser is obligated to honor and that may restrict the purchaser in some way from getting the full enjoyment of the property. An example is a restrictive covenant given to a neighbor that no dogs or cats would be kept on the property or that no building would exceed five metres in height in order not to spoil the view. These may be very important to a purchaser who was buying the land to erect a two-storey building or who was fond of pets.

Other restrictive covenants that may be important would be an obligation to construct within a certain time period or within a certain building scheme. On the other hand, a restrictive covenant not to keep sheep may not be too important. A restrictive covenant preventing a sale to any person based on race, religion, or sex is not enforceable.

The important thing is that the purchaser be aware of the contents of the restrictive covenant before accepting the interim agreement and agreeing to whatever restrictive covenants are registered against the property. If the wording is as set out above simply delete the two words, "restrictive covenants" by striking them out and initialling the deletion.

(b) Existing tenancies: this covenant may be quite acceptable if a revenue property is being purchased. However, if the purchaser immediately intends to move in after completion, it must be removed. This again can be done by striking out the two words and initialling them. There are two places where they may appear. First, in the covenant that is being discussed. Second, in the clause dealing with possession. This usually reads:

The purchaser to have possession of the property subject to existing tenancies at 12 noon on _____

To fix this clause, strike "subject to existing tenancies" and insert the word "vacant" immediately prior to the word "possession." Initial both changes. This removes the onus of ensuring the tenant vacates to the vendor. However, if the possession date is after the completion date so that it is not possible to make vacant possession a condition of closing (i.e., to hold up payment until vacant possession is given) the words "vacant and" should be added (and initialled) to the covenant starting "free and clear...."

(c) Reservations and exceptions in the original grant from the Crown: this means that the vendor cannot convey more than the Crown granted in the first place. In 99% of the cases this means mineral rights do not come with the land. These can be acquired separately, but until then it will not help you dream about finding a gold mine or an oil well on your property.

(d) Easements in favor of utilities and public authorities: these have already been discussed in chapter 3. Needless to say, it is important to know exactly what such easements allow and where they run.

(e) Encumbrances as set out above: this refers to something previously mentioned in the agreement. An example would be where the purchaser is assuming an existing mortgage. Here, of course, it is crucial to know the terms and conditions of such a mortgage before agreeing to accept it. What are the payments; when are they to be made; when is the mortgage due; what is the interest rate; is it assumable; does it allow prepayment and on what conditions; and so on.

The interim agreement should also contain two other provisions that are relatively new to the industry. These make conveyancing much easier on closing, especially if one of the parties wants to get out of the transaction.

The first provision is one that allows the purchaser's solicitor or notary to tender a trust cheque rather than cash on closing, and to rely on and use the mortgage funds to pay the purchase price, rather than forcing the purchaser to come up with cash before mortgage proceeds are available. The second provision assists the vendor by allowing title to be cleared from the sales proceeds, rather than forcing the vendor to clear title ahead of time from his or her own resources.

Other parts of the fine print provide for agreement on the type of documentation to be used to complete the transaction and a covenant by the parties that it be signed on or before the completion date.

There is also a proviso that specifically states that there are no warranties or representations other than those set out in the interim agreement, and they survive the closing date. That is, they are not subject to merger (explained in the following section).

Every warranty or representation on which a person wishes to rely must be written in the interim agreement. Therefore, if you have concerns about the roof, or wiring, or heating system, or whatever, obtain a written warranty in the interim agreement. If nothing else, it will serve to flush out items the vendor is reluctant to disclose. Be careful, however, about the wording. Vendors should not be reluctant to disclose past experiences, but should not, in the case of older homes, have to give warranties about the future performance of the house. Chapter 3, section **d.** considers the subject of warranties in greater depth.

Finally, the fine print provides a place to insert a date and a time. The offer is to remain until this time, and the vendor must accept it before then. This time line should be left relatively short, depending on the circumstances, so that it forces the vendor to make a decision. If too much time is given, the agent has no real lever to get the vendor to sign, and the vendor may just choose not to sign until the very last minute in the hope of getting a better offer.

10. Merger (The interim could become meaningless after registration)

This is a technical legal area which is important but still appears to be somewhat unsettled. The basic premise is that if there is a contract such as an interim agreement which is later to be "merged" into a deed or other document, the real completed contract between the parties is to be found in that deed or other document and not in the interim agreement. Once that final deed or document has been signed, the parties cannot look back to the previous contract.

Therefore, when an interim agreement specifies that the lot dimensions are 30 metres by 50 metres and this condition is not also mentioned in the deed, the purchaser cannot at a later stage sustain a claim for damages against the vendor when it is discovered that the property is only 30 metres by 45 metres.

The exceptions to the doctrine of merger appear to be when there is fraud or a mistake to such an extent that the parties get something entirely different from what they bargained for. The doctrine on merger applies in most instances to mere warranties and representations. Therefore, where it is desired that these warranties and representations continue after the actual conveyancing documents have been signed, the conveyancing documents should plainly specify these conditions. This can be done by stating plainly in the interim agreement and in the conveyancing documentation that the "warranties, representations, guarantees, promises, and agreements shall survive the completion date."

5

ALL ABOUT MORTGAGES

a. WHAT IS A MORTGAGE?

Most people who purchase a home, whether it is a fully or semi-detached unit, condominium, co-op, or trailer, require financial assistance. Sources of financial assistance can vary from a rich relative to a bank or trust company or from a sleazy loan shark to a government grant. Some of the more acceptable sources are discussed in the next chapter. However, before getting into that, some general things should be said about *mortgages*, as they are by far the most common means of raising the necessary funds to complete the purchase.

The mortgage relationship is really a debtor-creditor relationship. The word itself indicates this relationship, a "gage" being a pledge to ensure that an obligation will be fulfilled.

In the twelfth and thirteenth centuries, a transaction was either a mort-gage (dead pledge) or a vif-gage (live pledge). In a vif-gage, repayment depended on the profits of the land and was more of a partnership. In a mort-gage, repayment of the debt had no direct relationship to the profits of the land.

Today a mortgage is usually thought of as a loan of money from a money lender (mortgagee) to a money borrower (mortgagor) who owns land and provides it as security for the loan.

In British Columbia a mortgage document is registered in the appropriate Land Title Office as a charge against interest in the land that the borrower is mortgaging, although title of the property (or other interest in the property) remains with the borrower.

The conditions in a mortgage vary from mortgage document to mortgage document. Some mortgages require no payment until the time that they are to be paid off, while others require only interest payments and still others require both interest and principal payments. This last type of mortgage is called an amortized mortgage. (The conventional house mortgage is an amortized mortgage.) The principal balance owing under an amortized mortgage is reduced with each payment. If it takes 25 years to pay off the mortgage, the amortization period of the mortgage is 25 years.

This is not to be confused with the *term* of the mortgage. The term of the mortgage refers to the length of time that the lender will lend the money to the borrower. Thus a mortgage with a 25-year amortization and a 5-year term means that the money under the mortgage becomes due in 5 years, but if payments were allowed to continue beyond that term, the mortgage would become fully amortized over 25 years.

It used to be that when a conventional mortgage was granted, the term and amortization period both extended over 25 years. However, with the sharp rise in interest rates and the Canada Interest Act's statutory prepayment privilege after 5 years, it has now become common practice to grant terms not exceeding 5 years so that mortgage interest rates can be reviewed at least every 5 years.

If the borrower has made regular, prompt payments under the mortgage, the mortgage is usually allowed to continue past the due date at the then-current interest rate, which could be either higher or lower. A borrower who is not satisfied has the option of taking out a mortgage elsewhere, but should, before doing so, carefully check the interest rate.

The most expensive part of acquiring a house is, in most instances, not the capital cost of the house, but the interest expense on the mortgage. The interest expense alone on, for instance, a $35 000 mortgage at 10% interest amortized over 25 years would be $58 924, making the total amount that would have to be repaid $93 924. Please note that the interest expense is directly proportional to the loan amount. Therefore if instead we were discussing a $70 000 mortgage (i.e., 2 x $35 000) then the interest expense would be 2 x $58 924 = $117 848 and the total amount that would have to be repaid would be 2 x $93 924 = $187 848.

The same $35 000 mortgage written at 11% interest would require a total repayment of $101 067 of which $66 067 would be pure interest expense. A 1% increase in the interest rate on a $35 000 mortgage means an additional interest expense of $7 143 over 25 years, so do not take the interest rate lightly!

What makes that enormous expense even worse is that mortgage interest on a home must be paid with *after-tax money*. This is in sharp contrast to our neighbors to the south who, besides having to spend less on comparable housing, and having lower mortgage interest rates, are able to use the interest expense as a deduction for tax purposes.

If you can't do anything about the mortgage rate, you can still save a tremendous amount of money by paying attention to the amortization period. Most mortgage companies will base their repayment of the mortgage on a 25-year amortization period. If you are able to increase your monthly mortgage payment slightly, the 25 years that it would take you to repay the mortgage can be reduced substantially, and the interest savings are staggering. For instance, a $50 000 mortgage at 12% interest amortized over 25 years requires payments of $515.95 per month. If the amortization period were based on 20 years, the payment would amount to $540.49, or an increase of $24.54 per month. This slight increase in the payments would shorten the mortgage period by 60 payments of $515.95 or $30 909.

Another $30 000 can be saved by increasing the payment from $540.49 to $590.81. This would make a 15-year amortization and increase the savings over the 25-year amortization by a total of $61 818.00. These savings are, of course, strictly savings on interest that would otherwise have accrued on the mortgage and are even greater for larger principal amounts, or higher interest rates. You can work out other examples by using Table #1 in chapter 6.

With the recent advent of high fluctuating interest rates, the mortgage industry has had to change many customary business methods and this has caused some new products to be developed while some old standby products have been drastically altered, or even ceased to exist. Some of these innovations include semi-monthly or even weekly mortgage payments.

The mortgage industry operates by borrowing money on term deposits for set periods of time at agreed upon rates and then lending that same money out on roughly matching time periods at a mark-up of 2% to 3% to cover overhead and risk. People are more reluctant to lend their money on a longer term basis, so it is more difficult to get longer term mortgages. That is the reason mortgages with one- and two-year terms have become so common.

The variable rate mortgage is an innovation that attempts to address the problems of the fluctuating interest rates. Under the terms of the variable rate mortgage, the interest rate charged in any month is the current rate for that month. It may be up or down from the previous month, but the amount of the payment stays the same. Consequently, in one month the payment may not be enough to cover the interest charges, while in another month it may be more than adequate for both interest and a reduction in principal. This type of mortgage makes it easier for the mortgage company to match short-term funds while at the same time giving the borrower a fixed payment and cash flow certainty.

b. THE CONTENTS OF A MORTGAGE

By the Land Title Amendment Act 1989, which became effective in April, 1990, all freehold transfers, all mortgages, and general conveyancing documents filed with the Land Title Office must be submitted in prescribed form and completed and executed in the prescribed manner. This was required in order to computerize the office so that documents can be processed, stored, retrieved, and accessed electronically.

To achieve this for mortgages, for example, a general "term and condition" form is signed by the mortgagor which automatically adapts a standard form of mortgage on file in the Land Title Office (although it is possible to file a specialized mortgage with the form). This form also sets out the terms and conditions of the mortgage and must be signed by the mortgagor in front of a lawyer or notary public. Sample #5 illustrates a general mortgage form. You can see that this form lists and identifies the parties, states the amount that is being borrowed, details the legal description of the property taken as security, summarizes the terms of repayment of the loan, and gives disclosure of the Canada Interest Act rate.

This is required because in an amortized mortgage, the Canada Interest Act requires that, where payments of principal money and interest are blended, no interest shall be chargeable or recoverable on any part of the principal unless the mortgage contains a statement showing separately the amount of the principal and the rate of interest on an annual or semi-annual basis.

Unless otherwise indicated, the mortgage terms adapted by the general form are those reproduced as Sample #6. A copy of these mortgage terms must be given to the mortgagor at the time when the general form is signed. The most important parts of the mortgage terms for the lender are the parts dealing with remedies if the borrower defaults in the repayment of the debt. These are, however, discussed further in chapter 10.

Among other important provisions in the mortgage terms is the covenant that the borrower will insure the building. This is a reasonable clause, as the building, in all likelihood, forms

---

LAND TITLE ACT
FORM B
(Section 219.1)

**Province of
British Columbia**

MORTGAGE – PART 1   (This area for Land Title Office use)   PAGE 1 of _____ pages

1. APPLICATION: (Name, address, phone number and signature of applicant, applicant's solicitor or agent)

    Diane Lawyer of Best & Knowitall, Barristers & Solicitors,
  1234 – 5th Street, Vancouver, B.C. V1A 3Z2   681-0123

2. PARCEL IDENTIFIER(S) AND LEGAL DESCRIPTION(S) OF THE MORTGAGED LAND: *
   (PID)   (LEGAL DESCRIPTION)

012 345 678   Lot 1, Block 2, Group 3, N.W.D., Plan 111222

3. BORROWER(S) (MORTGAGOR(S)): (including postal address(es) and postal code(s)) *

   FELIX FELINE and MAGGIE FELINE, both of 23 Kitty Lane,
  Vancouver, British Columbia, V2A 7A6

4. LENDER(S) (MORTGAGEE(S)): (including occupation(s), postal address(es) and postal code(s)) *

   FRIENDLY MORTGAGE COMPANY LTD., a B.C. Corporation having
  an office at 999 West Hastings Street, Vancouver, B.C., V6C 2W2

5. PAYMENT PROVISIONS: **

			Y	M	D
(a) Principal Amount: $ 125 000.00	(b) Interest Rate: 12% per annum	(c) Interest Adjustment Date:	9–	05	01
(d) Interest Calculation Period: semi-annually	(e) Payment Dates: 1st day of each month	(f) First Payment Date:	9–	06	01
(g) Amount of each periodic payment: $1 250.00	(h) *Interest Act* (Canada) Statement: The equivalent rate of interest calculated half yearly not in advance is 12 % per annum.	(i) Last Payment Date:	9–	04	01
(j) Assignment of Rents which the applicant wants registered? YES ☐ NO ☒ If YES, page and paragraph number:	(k) Place of payment: at address set out in Item 4	(l) Balance Due Date:	9–	05	01

*   If space insufficient, enter "SEE SCHEDULE" and attach schedule in Form E.
** If space in any box insufficient, enter "SEE SCHEDULE" and attach schedule in Form E.

MORTGAGE – PART 1

6. MORTGAGE contains
floating charge on land?   YES ☐   NO ☒

7. MORTGAGE secures a current
or running account?   YES ☐   NO ☒

8. INTEREST MORTGAGED:
Freehold   ☒
Other (specify)   ☐*

9. MORTGAGE TERMS:

Part 2 of this mortgage consists of (select one only):
(a) Prescribed Standard Mortgage Terms   ☒
(b) Filed Standard Mortgage Terms   ☐   D.F. Number:
(c) Express Mortgage Terms   ☐   (annexed to this mortgage as Part 2)

A selection of (a) or (b) includes any additional or modified terms referred to in Item 10 or in a schedule annexed to this mortgage.

10. ADDITIONAL OR MODIFIED TERMS: *

N/A

11. PRIOR ENCUMBRANCES PERMITTED BY LENDER: *

a) SRW K98764

b) Easement L32109

12. EXECUTION(S): ** This mortgage charges the Borrower's interest in the land mortgaged as security for payment of all money due and performance of all obligations in accordance with the mortgage terms referred to in Item 9 and the Borrower(s) and every other signatory agree(s) to be bound by, and acknowledge(s) receipt of a true copy of, those terms.

Officer Signature(s)	Execution Date			Borrower(s) Signature(s)
	Y	M	D	

Officer Signature
DIANE LAWYER, Solicitor
(as to both signatures)   9- 04-20
1234 - 5th Street
Vancouver, B.C.
V1A 3Z2

Borrower Signature
FELIX FELINE

Borrower Signature
MAGGIE FELINE

OFFICER CERTIFICATION:
Your signature constitutes a representation that you are a solicitor, notary public or other person authorized by the *Evidence Act*, R.S.B.C. 1979, c. 116, to take affidavits for use in British Columbia and certifies the matters set out in Part 5 of the *Land Title Act* as they pertain to the execution of this instrument.

*   If space insufficient, enter "SEE SCHEDULE" and attach schedule in Form E.
**   If space insufficient, continue executions on additional page(s) in Form D.

PRESCRIBED STANDARD MORTGAGE TERMS

These mortgage terms are considered to be included in and form a part of every mortgage which incorporates prescribed standard mortgage terms, either by an election in the mortgage form or by operation of law.

INTERPRETATION

1. (1) In these mortgage terms

"Borrower" means the person or persons named in the mortgage form as a borrower

"Borrower mailing address" means the postal address of the borrower set out in the mortgage form or the most recent postal address provided in a written notice given by the borrower to the lender under these mortgage terms

"Borrower's promises and agreements" means any one or more of the borrower's obligations, promises and agreements contained in this mortgage

"court" means a court or judge having jurisdiction in any matter arising out of this mortgage

"covenantor" means a person who signs the mortgage form as a covenantor

"default" includes each of the events of default listed in section 7(1)

"interest" means interest at the interest rate shown on the mortgage form

"interest adjustment date" means the interest adjustment date shown on the mortgage form

"interest calculation period" means the period or periods for the calculation of interest shown on the mortgage form

"interest rate" means the interest rate shown on the mortgage form

"land" means all the borrower's present and future interest in the land described in the mortgage form including every incidental right, benefit or privilege attaching to that land or running with it and all buildings and improvements that are now or later constructed on or made to that land

"lease" means the leasehold interest, if any, of the borrower referred to in the mortgage form

"lender" means the person or persons named in the mortgage form as a lender and includes any person to whom the lender transfers this mortgage

"lender mailing address" means the postal address shown on the mortgage form or the most recent postal address provided in a written notice given by the lender to the borrower under these mortgage terms

"loan payment" means the amount of each periodic payment shown on the mortgage form

"maturity date" means the balance due date shown on the mortgage form and is the date on which all unpaid mortgage money becomes due and payable, or such earlier date on which the lender can lawfully require payment of the mortgage money

"mortgage form" means Form B under the Land Title (Transfer Forms) Regulation and all schedules and addenda to Form B

"Mortgage money" means the principal amount, interest and any other money owed by the borrower under this mortgage, the payment of which is secured by this mortgage

"payment date" means each payment date commencing on the first payment date shown on the mortgage form

"place of payment" means the place of payment shown on the mortgage form or any other place specified in a written notice given by the lender to the borrower under these mortgage terms

"principal amount" means the amount of money shown as the principal amount on the mortgage form as reduced by payments made by the borrower from time to time, or increased by the advance or readvance of money to the borrower by the lender from time to time, and includes all money that is later added to the principal amount under these mortgage terms

"receiver" means a receiver or receiver manager appointed by the lender under this mortgage

"taxes" means all taxes, rates and assessments of every kind which are payable by any person in connection with this mortgage, the land or its use and occupation, or arising out of any transaction between the borrower and the lender, but does not include the lender's income tax

"this mortgage" means the combination of the mortgage form and these mortgage terms.

(2) In this mortgage the singular includes the plural and vice versa.

What this mortgage does

2. (1) In return for the lender agreeing to lend the principal amount to the borrower, the borrower grants and mortgages the land to the lender as security for repayment of the mortgage money and for performance of all the borrower's promises and agreements.

(2) If the interest mortgaged is described in the mortgage form as a leasehold interest, the grant in subsection (1) shall be construed as a charge of the unexpired term of the lease less the last month of that term.

(3) This means that —

    (a)   this mortgage shall be a charge on the land, and

    (b)   the borrower releases to the lender all the borrower's claim to the land until the borrower has paid the mortgage money to the lender, in accordance with these mortgage terms, and has performed all of the borrower's promises and agreements.

(4) The borrower may continue to remain in possession of the land as long as the borrower performs all of the borrower's promises and agreements.

(5) When the borrower has paid the mortgage money and performed all the borrower's promises and agreements under this mortgage and the lender has no obligation to make any further advances or readvances, the lender will no longer be entitled to enforce any rights under this mortgage and the borrower will be entitled, at the borrower's cost, to receive a discharge of this mortgage. The discharge must be signed by the lender and must be registered by the borrower in the land title office to cancel the registration of this mortgage against the land.

INTEREST

3. (1) Interest is chargeable on the mortgage money and is payable by the borrower.

(2) Interest is not payable in advance. This means that interest must be earned before it is payable.

(3) Interest on advances or readvances of the principal amount starts on the date and on the amount of each advance or readvance and accrues on the principal amount until the borrower has paid all the mortgage money.

(4) Interest payable on any part of the principal amount advanced before the interest adjustment date is due and payable to the lender on the interest adjustment date.

(5) At the end of each interest calculation period, unpaid accrued interest will be added to the principal amount and bear interest. This is known as compound interest.

PAYMENT OF THE MORTGAGE MONEY

4. The borrower promises to pay the mortgage money to the lender at the place of payment in accordance with the payment provisions set out in the mortgage form and these mortgage terms.

PROMISES OF THE BORROWER

5. (1) the borrower promises —

(a) to pay all taxes when they are due and to send to the lender at the place of payment, or at any other place the lender requires, all notices of taxes which the borrower receives,

(b) if the lender requires the borrower to do so, to pay to the lender —

(i) on each payment date the amount of money estimated by the lender to be sufficient to permit the lender to pay the taxes when they are due, and

(ii) any money in addition to the money already paid towards taxes so that the lender will be able to pay the taxes in full,

(c) to apply for all government grants, assistance and rebates in respect of taxes,

(d) to comply with all terms and conditions of any charge or encumbrance that ranks ahead of this mortgage,

(e) to keep all buildings and improvements which form part of the land in good condition and to repair them as the lender reasonably requires,

(f) to sign any other document that the lender reasonably requires to ensure that payment of the mortgage money is secured by this mortgage or by any other document the borrower has agreed to give as security,

(g) not to do anything that has the effect of reducing the value of the land,

(h) not to tear down any building or part of a building which forms part of the land,

(i) not to make any alteration or improvement to any building which forms part of the land without the written consent of the lender,

(j) if the borrower has rented the land to a tenant, to keep, if required by the lender, records of all rents received and of all expenses paid by the borrower in connection with the land and, at least annually, have a statement of revenue and expenses for the land prepared by a professional accountant if the lender requires and to give a copy of the statement to the lender if the lender requires the borrower to do so,

(k) to insure and keep insured against the risk of fire and other risks and losses that the lender ask the borrower to insure against, with an insurance company licensed to do business in British Columbia, all buildings and improvements on the land to their full insurable value on a replacement cost basis and to pay all insurance premiums when due,

(l) to send a copy of each insurance policy and renewal certificate to the lender at the place of payment,

(m) to pay all of the lender's costs, including legal fees on a solicitor and client basis, to —

    (i) prepare and register this mortgage, including all necessary steps to advance and secure the mortgage money and to report to the lender,

    (ii) collect mortgage money,

    (iii) enforce the terms of this mortgage, including efforts to compel the borrower to perform the borrower's promises and agreements,

    (iv) do anything which the borrower has promised to do but has not done, and

    (v) prepare and give the borrower a discharge of this mortgage when the borrower has paid all money due under this mortgage and the borrower wants it to be discharged,

(n) if the lender requires the borrower to do so, to —

    (i) give the lender in each year post-dated cheques for all loan payments due for that year and for taxes, and

    (ii) arrange for all loan payments to be made by pre-authorizing chequing,

(o) to pay any money which, if not paid, would result in a default under any charge or encumbrance having priority over this mortgage or which might result in the sale of the land if not paid, and

(p) to pay and cause to be discharged any charges or encumbrances described in subsection (2)(b) which are not prior encumbrances permitted by the lender under this mortgage.

(2) The borrower declares to the lender that —

(a) the borrower owns the land and has the right to mortgage the land to the lender,

(b) the borrower's title to the land is subject only to —

    (i) those charges and encumbrances that are registered in the land title office at the time the borrower signed the mortgage form, and

    (ii) any unregistered charges and encumbrances that the lender has agreed to in writing, and

(c) subject to paragraph (b), the borrower —

    (i) has not given any other charge or encumbrance against the land, and

    (ii) has no knowledge of any other claim against the land.

(3) The insurance policy or policies required by subsection (1)(k) shall contain a mortgage clause approved by the lender that states that payment of any loss shall be made to the lender at the place of payment or any other place the lender requires and, if this mortgage is not a first mortgage, the amount of any payment made by the insurance company shall be paid to the borrower's lenders in the order of their priorities.

(4) The borrower gives up any statutory right to require the insurance proceeds to be applied in any particular manner.

AGREEMENTS BETWEEN THE BORROWER AND THE LENDER

6. (1) The lender will use the money paid to the lender under section 5(1)(b) to pay taxes unless there is a default in which case the lender may apply the money in payment of the mortgage money.

(2) By this mortgage the borrower grants and mortgages any additional or greater interest in the land that the borrower may later acquire.

(3) Any money paid to the lender under this mortgage shall —

    (a) prior to a default, be applied first in payment of interest, secondly in payment of the principal amount and thirdly in payment of all other money owed by the borrower under this mortgage, and

    (b) after a default, be applied in any manner the lender chooses.

(4) The lender may at any reasonable time inspect the land and any buildings and improvements which form part of it.

(5) If the lender takes possession of the land the lender shall not be responsible for maintaining and preserving the land and need only account to the borrower for any money which the lender actually receives in connection with this mortgage or the land.

(6) The lender may spend money to perform any of the borrower's promises and agreements which the borrower has not performed and any money so spent shall be added to the principal amount, bear interest from the date that the money was so spent, and be immediately due and payable to the lender.

(7) If the borrower wants to give any notice to the lender, the borrower must do so by having it delivered to the lender personally or by sending it by registered or certified mail to the lender mailing address or to any other address later specified in writing by the lender to the borrower.

(8) If the lender wants to give any notice to the borrower, the lender must do so by having it delivered to the borrower personally or by sending it by registered or certified mail to the borrower mailing address or to any other address later specified in writing by the borrower to the lender.

(9) Any notice sent by mail is considered to have been received 5 days after it is mailed.

(10) Any notice to be given by the borrower to the lender or vice versa during mail strike or disruption must be delivered rather than sent by mail.

(11) The borrower is not released from the borrower's promises and agreements only because the borrower sells the land.

(12) If the borrower has mortgaged anything else to the lender better to secure payment of the mortgage money, the lender may take all lawful proceedings under any of the mortgages in any order that the lender chooses.

(13) The lender does not have to advance or readvance the principal amount or the rest or any further part of the principal amount to the borrower unless the lender wants to even though —

    (a) the borrower has signed this mortgage,

    (b) this mortgage is registered in the land title office, or

    (c) the lender has advanced to the borrower part of the principal amount.

(14) The lender may deduct from any advance of the principal amount —

    (a)   any taxes that are due,

    (b)   any interest that is due and payable to the date of the advance,

    (c)   the legal fees and disbursements to prepare and register this mortgage including other necessary steps to advance and secure the mortgage money and to report to the lender, and

    (d)   any insurance premium.

(15) The lender's right of consolidation applies to this mortgage and to any other mortgages given by the borrower to the lender. This means that if the borrower has mortgaged other property to the lender the borrower will not have the right, after default, to pay off this mortgage or any mortgage of other property unless the borrower pays the lender all money owed by the borrower under this mortgage and all of the mortgages of other property.

DEFAULTS

7. (1) A default occurs under this mortgage if —

    (a)   the borrower breaks any of the borrower's promises and agreements,

    (b)   the borrower breaks any promise or agreement which the borrower has made to the lender in a mortgage of any other land or other property or in any other agreement the borrower has made with the lender even though the borrower may not have broken any of the borrower's promises and agreements,

    (c)   the borrower becomes bankrupt,

    (d)   the land is abandoned or is left unoccupied for 30 or more consecutive days,

    (e)   the land or any part of it is expropriated,

    (f)   the borrower sells or agrees to sell all or any part of the land or if the borrower leases it or any part of it without the prior written consent of the lender,

    (g)   the borrower gives another mortgage of the land to someone other than the lender without the prior written consent of the lender,

    (h)   the borrower does not discharge any judgment registered in the land title office against the land within 30 days after receiving notice of its registration, or

    (i)   the borrower allows any claim of builders lien to remain undischarged on title to the land for more than 30 days unless the borrower —

        (i) diligently disputes the validity of the claim by taking all necessary legal steps to do so,

        (ii) gives reasonable security to the lender to pay the claim in full if it is found to be valid, and

        (iii) authorizes the lender to use the security to pay the lien in full.

(2) If a default occurs under this mortgage, it will have the same effect as though a default had occurred under any other mortgage or agreement between the borrower and the lender.

CONSEQUENCES OF A DEFAULT

8.(1) If a default occurs, all the mortgage money then owing to the lender will, if the lender chooses, at once become due and payable.

(2) If a default occurs the lender may, in any order that the lender chooses, do any one or more of the following:

   (a)   demand payment of all the mortgage money;

   (b)   sue the borrower for the amount of money due;

   (c)   take proceedings and any other legal steps to compel the borrower to keep the borrower's promises and agreements;

   (d)   enter upon and take possession of the land;

   (e)   sell the land and other property by public auction or private sale, or lease the land on terms decided by the lender —

      (i) on 30 days notice to the borrower if the default has continued for 30 days, or

      (ii) without notice to the borrower if the default has continued for 60 days or more;

   (f)   apply to the court for an order that the land be sold on terms approved by the court;

   (g)   apply to the court to foreclose the borrower's interest in the land so that when the court makes its final order of foreclosure the borrower's interest in the land will be absolutely vested in and belong to the lender;

   (h)   appoint a receiver of the land;

   (i)   enter upon and take possession of the land without the permission of anyone and make any arrangements the lender considers necessary to —

      (i) inspect, lease, collect rents or manage the land,

      (ii) complete the construction of any building on the land, or

      (iii) repair any building on the land;

   (j)   take whatever action is necessary to take, recover and keep possession of the land.

(3) Nothing in subsection (2) affects the jurisdiction of the court.

(4) If the lender sells the land by public auction or by private sale the lender will use the amount received from the sale to pay —

   (a)   any real estate agent's commission,

   (b)   all adjustments usually made on the sale of land,

   (c)   all of the lender's expenses and costs described in subsection (6), and

   (d)   the mortgage money,

and will pay any surplus —

   (e)   according to an order of the court if the land is sold by an order of the court, or

   (f)   to the borrower if the land is sold other than by an order of the court.

(5) If the money available to pay the mortgage money after payment of the commission, adjustments and expenses referred to in subsection(4)(a) to (c) is not sufficient to pay all the mortgage money, the borrower will pay to the lender on demand the amount of the deficiency.

(6) The borrower will pay to the lender on demand all expenses and costs incurred by the lender in enforcing this mortgage. These expenses and costs include the lender's cost of taking and keeping possession of the land, the cost of the time and services of the lender or the lender's employees for so doing, the lender's legal fees and disbursements on a solicitor and client basis, unless the court allows legal fees and disbursements be paid on a different basis, and all other costs and expenses incurred by the lender to protect the lender's interest under this mortgage. These expenses and costs will be added to the principal amount, be payable on demand and bear interest until they are fully paid.

(7) If the lender obtains judgment against the borrower as a result of a default, the remedies described in subsection (2) may continue to be used by the lender to compel the borrower to perform the borrower's promises and agreements. The lender will continue to be entitled to receive interest on the mortgage money until the judgment is paid in full.

(8) If the lender does not exercise any of the lender's rights on the happening of a default or does not ask the borrower to cure it, the lender is not prevented from later compelling the borrower to cure that default or exercising any of those rights in connection with that default or any later default of the same of any other kind.

CONSTRUCTION OF BUILDING OR IMPROVEMENTS

9. (1) The borrower will not construct, alter or add to any buildings or improvements on the land without the prior written consent of the lender, and then only in accordance with accepted construction standards, building codes and municipal or government requirements and plans and specifications approved by the lender.

(2) If this mortgage is intended to finance any construction, alteration or addition, the lender may make advances of the principal amount to the borrower based on the progress of construction. The lender will decide whether or not any advances will be made, the amount of the advances, and when they will be made.

LEASEHOLD MORTGAGE

10. (1) This section applies if the interest mortgaged shown in the mortgage form is or includes a leasehold interest.

(2) The borrower represents to the lender that —

    (a) the lease is owned by the borrower subject only to those charges and encumbrances that are registered in the land title office at the time the borrower signs the mortgage form,

    (b) the lease is in good standing,

    (c) the borrower has complied with all the borrower's promises and agreements contained in the lease,

    (d) the borrower has paid all rent that is due and payable under the lease,

    (e) the lease is not in default, and

    (f) the borrower has the right to mortgage the lease to the lender.

(3) The borrower will —

    (a)   comply with the lease and not do anything that would cause the lease to be terminated,

    (b)   immediately give to the lender a copy of any notice or request received from the landlord,

    (c)   immediately notify the lender if the landlord advises the borrower of the landlord's intention to terminate the lease before the term expires, and

    (d)   sign any other document the lender requires to ensure that any greater interest in the land that is acquired by the borrower is charged by this mortgage.

(4) Any default under the lease is a default under this mortgage.

(5) The borrower promises the lender that the borrower will not, without first obtaining the written consent of the lender,

    (a)   surrender or terminate the lease, or

    (b)   agree to change the terms of the lease.

(6) The lender may perform any promise or agreement of the borrower under the lease.

(7) Nothing done by the lender under this section will make the lender a mortgagee in possession.

RECEIVER

11. (1) The borrower appoints both the lender and any agent of the lender as the borrower's attorney to appoint a receiver of the land.

(2) The lender or the lender's agent may, if any default happens, appoint a receiver of the land and the receiver —

    (a)   will be the borrower's agent and the borrower will be solely responsible for the receiver's acts or omissions,

    (b)   has power, either in the borrower's name or in the name of the lender, to demand, recover and receive income from the land and start and carry on any action or court proceeding to collect that income,

    (c)   may give receipts for income which the receiver receives,

    (d)   may carry on any business which the borrower conducted on the land,

    (e)   may lease or sublease the land or any part of it on terms and conditions that the receiver chooses,

    (f)   may complete the construction of or repair any building or improvement on the land,

    (g)   may take possession of all or part of the land,

    (h)   may manage the land and maintain it in good condition,

    (i)   has the power to perform, in whole or in part, the borrower's promises and agreements, and

    (j)   has the power to do anything that, in the receiver's opinion, will maintain and preserve the land or will increase or preserve the value or income potential of the land or the borrower's business on the land.

(3) From income received the receiver may do any of the following in any order the receiver chooses:

  (a) retain a commission of 5% of the gross income or any higher commission approved by the court;

  (b) retain enough money to pay or recover the cost to collect the income and to cover other disbursements;

  (c) pay all taxes and the cost of maintaining the land in good repair, completing the construction of any building or improvement on the land, supplying goods, utilities and services to the land and taking steps to preserve the land from damage by weather, vandalism or any other cause;

  (d) pay any money that might, if not paid, result in a default under any charge or encumbrance having priority over this mortgage or that might result in the sale of the land if not paid;

  (e) pay taxes in connection with anything the receiver is entitled to do under this mortgage;

  (f) pay interest to the lender that is due and payable;

  (g) pay all or part of the principal amount to the lender whether or not it is due and payable;

  (h) pay any other money owed by the borrower under this mortgage;

  (i) pay insurance premiums.

(4) The receiver may borrow money for the purpose of doing anything the receiver is authorized to do.

(5) Any money borrowed by the receiver, and any interest charged on the money and all the costs of borrowing, will be added to and be part of the mortgage money.

(6) A receiver appointed by the lender may be removed by the lender and the lender may appoint another in the receiver's place.

(7) The commission and disbursements of the receiver will be a charge on the land and will bear interest at the interest rate.

(8) Nothing done by the receiver under this section will make the lender a mortgagee in possession.

STRATA LOT PROVISIONS

12. (1) This section applies if the land described in the mortgage form is or becomes a strata lot created under the *Condominium Act*.

(2) The borrower will fulfill all of the borrower's obligations as a strata lot owner under the *Condominium Act* and the bylaws, rules and regulations of the strata corporation and will pay all money owed by the borrower to the strata corporation.

(3) The borrower gives to the lender the right to vote for the borrower under the bylaws of the strata corporation, but the lender is not required to do so or to attend or vote at any meeting or to protect the borrower's interest.

(4) At the request of the lender, the borrower will give the lender copies of all notices, financial statements and other documents given by the strata corporation to the borrower.

(5) The borrower appoints the lender to be the borrower's agent to inspect or obtain copies of any records or other documents of the strata corporation that the borrower is entitled to inspect or obtain.

(6) If the strata corporation transfers, charges or adds to the common property, or amends its bylaws without the consent of the lender, and if, in the lender's opinion, the value of the land is reduced, the mortgage money shall, at the lender's option, immediately become due and payable to the lender on demand.

(7) Nothing done by the lender under this section will make the lender a mortgagee in possession.

SUBDIVISION

13. (1) If the land is subdivided —

    (a)   this mortgage will charge each subdivided lot as security for payment of all the mortgage money, and

    (b)   the lender is not required to discharge this mortgage as a charge on any of the subdivided lots unless all the mortgage money is paid.

(2) Even though the lender is not required to discharge any subdivided lot from this mortgage, the lender may agree to do so in return for payment of all or a part of the mortgage money. If the lender discharges a subdivided lot, this mortgage will continue to charge the subdivided lot or lots that have not been discharged.

CURRENT AND RUNNING ACCOUNT

14. If the mortgage form states that this mortgage secures a current or running account, the lender may, on one or more occasions, advance or readvance all or part of the principal amount and this mortgage —

    (a)   will be security for payment for the principal amount as advanced and readvanced and for all other money payable to the lender under this mortgage,

    (b)   will not be considered to have been redeemed only because —

        (i) the advances and readvances made to the borrower have been repaid, or

        (ii) the accounts of the borrower with the lender cease to be in debit, and

    (c)   remains effective security for further advances and readvances until the borrower has received a discharge of this mortgage.

COVENANTOR'S PROMISES AND AGREEMENTS

15. (1) As the lender would not have agreed to lend the principal amount to the borrower without the promises of the covenantor and in consideration of the lender advancing all or part of the principal amount to the borrower at the request of the covenantor, the covenantor promises —

    (a)   to pay all the mortgage money when due, and

    (b)   to keep and perform all the borrower's promises and agreements.

(2) The covenantor agrees that, with or without notice, the following shall in no way affect any of the promises of the covenantor or the liability of the covenantor to the lender:

    (a)   a discharge of the land or any part of the land from this mortgage;

    (b)   any disregard or waiver of a default;

    (c)   the giving of extra time to the borrower to —

        (i) do something that the borrower has agreed to do, or

        (ii) cure a default.

    (d)   any other dealing between the borrower and the lender that concerns this mortgage or the land.

(3) All the covenantor's promises shall be binding on the covenantor until all the mortgage money is fully paid to the lender.

(4) The covenantor is a primary debtor to the same extent as if the covenantor had signed this mortgage as a borrower and is not merely a guarantor or a surety, and the covenantor's promises and agreements are joint and several with the borrower's promises and agreements. This means that the covenantor and the borrower are both liable to perform all the borrower's promises and agreements.

(5) If more than one person signs the mortgage form as covenantor, the promises are both joint and several.

GENERAL

16. (1) This mortgage binds the borrower and the covenantor and their successors, executors, administrators and assigns.

(2) Each person who signs this mortgage as a borrower is jointly and severally liable for all of the borrower's promises and agreements as though each such borrower had been the only borrower to sign.

(3) If any part of this mortgage is not enforceable all other parts will remain in effect and be enforceable against the borrower and any covenantor.

the major part of the security, and the lender wants to have some protection against disaster.

When insurance is taken out, the lender will probably require that the policy contain a standard mortgage clause in which the insurance company agrees not to cancel the contract unless it gives adequate notice to the lender. The lender will also want the insurance policy to contain a clause that in the event of a claim under the policy, the lender will be paid before any proceeds are paid to the owner.

Another little item that protects the lender's security is a clause where the borrower promises to keep the land and buildings in good condition and repair. Unless this clause is complied with, the lender will again be able to foreclose.

It should also be noted that the terms of repayment are very important. Unless the mortgage specifically grants the borrower the right to prepay, the mortgage would in a mortgage with a five-year term, be a contract for five years and the borrower would not be able to repay the mortgage before that date. This is the subject of the next section.

c. PRIVILEGES

As mentioned before, many mortgages do not contain prepayment privileges. This is understandable, especially as far as the conventional mortgage lenders such as banks, trust companies, and life insurance companies are concerned. The money that these companies lend on mortgages is usually the money that other people have left on deposit with them and on which they have contracted to pay a certain rate of interest.

Therefore, if Friendly Trust Company had accepted money from Mrs. Lilly O. Lady on a five-year trust certificate paying interest at 10% per annum and had loaned that money out on a mortgage paying 11½% also on a five-year term, Friendly Trust would be very upset if the borrower had the privilege of prepaying the mortgage when the rates dropped to 9%, as Friendly Trust would still be under an obligation to pay 10% to Mrs. Lilly O. Lady.

At the same time, the fact that prepayment can be barred can cause real hardship to the borrower. Consider, for instance, Mr. I.M. Stuck who could not sell his house because he could not find any purchasers willing to assume his old mortgage as it did not suit their requirements, or pay off the mortgage so that purchasers could arrange their own mortgages.

From the borrower's point of view, it pays to shop around and/or negotiate the prepayment privileges. Prepayment clauses vary greatly from institution to institution. Even the ones that do allow prepayment stipulate that the borrower must pay an interest "penalty" for such a privilege. There are only a very few (usually with a credit union — although this has changed in the last couple of years) that allow the borrower to prepay the mortgage at any time without penalty. Others require the borrower to pay anywhere from one to, say, six months' penalty interest in the amount being prepaid. Still others will allow, for example, a prepayment of 10% of the outstanding principal without penalty on every anniversary date of the mortgage.

Even these limited rights of prepayment can be extremely precious if they can be taken advantage of. In a previous section we discussed the possibility of increasing the payments under the mortgage, thereby shortening the amortization period. Five years could save in excess of $30 000 on a $50 000 mortgage! These, or even better, results can be obtained through a limited prepayment privilege. For instance, for the mortgages that allow an annual prepayment privilege of up to 10% on original principal with a minimum of $500, and where even a minimum of $500 is taken advantage of, you would, on a $50 000 mortgage, be able to reduce the amortization period from 25 years to an effective amortization period of approximately 17 years. The savings would amount to approximately $49 000. Pay attention to these things; they are important!

Another privilege a mortgagor should give some consideration to is the right to renew the mortgage on its maturity or expiry date, that is, the date that the lender is entitled to demand payment of the money outstanding in full.

Provided the mortgage company has had no problems with the borrower, it will, in many instances, offer to extend the terms of the mortgage at the prevailing rate of interest.

However, unless the mortgage contains a clause granting the privilege of renewal, the lender could demand the payment of, and the borrower would be required to pay, the mortgage in full on the maturity date.

Also, if the borrower did not have the available cash to repay the mortgage when it became due, he or she could be forced to attempt to obtain a new mortgage from another company and would again have to pay all the associated costs in connection with arranging a new mortgage.

There is another privilege to keep in mind if you are arranging a second or third mortgage. This privilege is one to be negotiated with the lender of the second or third mortgage and applies in cases where the maturity date of the secondary financing is *after* the maturity date of the first mortgage.

This "replacement" privilege would permit the borrower to replace the primary financing up to a certain level on certain terms. An illustration of the problems that can be created where such a privilege has not been obtained would be the case of Fred Flounder.

Fred Flounder's first mortgage became due on June 30, 199-, at which time he owed $25 000. Knowing this, Fred Flounder had been able to arrange a new first mortgage from the Friendly Loan Company on very advantageous terms — also for the amount of $25 000. His second mortgage was, however, held by Sam Shark and did not contain a privilege clause allowing Fred Flounder to substitute the Friendly Loan Company mortgage for his old mortgage with Sam. Sam knew that:

(a) The repayment of Fred's old mortgage and sub-
    sequent discharge of a mortgage in the Land Title Office would automatically elevate Sam's mortgage to a first mortgage.

(b) The registration of the Friendly Loan Company's new mortgage, without the consent of Sam, could be registered only as a second mortgage.

(c) The Friendly Loan Company was prepared to grant only a first mortgage.

(d) Fred's second mortgage was only 12%, but second mortgage rates had now moved up to 18% (and Sam wanted his money back).

(e) Fred's second mortgage contained a prepayment privilege allowing Fred to pay out the second mortgage on payment of six months' additional interest as a bonus.

(f) Fred Flounder did not have sufficient funds to pay out the second mortgage.

Needless to say, in these circumstances, Fred Flounder has little choice but to go along with Sam Shark's proposal of having Shark's mortgage paid out with a six months' interest penalty and then having that same mortgage rewritten and reregistered at 18% interest.

Fred Flounder could, of course, have avoided this situation if he had, at the time he took out the mortgage, negotiated a "replacement" privilege with Sam Shark. This privilege is usually not too difficult to obtain, provided that the borrower is willing to allow any increase in the first mortgage to be paid in reduction of the second mortgage, so that the second lender's equity is at all times protected. Thus, if Fred

Flounder had been able to obtain $30 000 from the Friendly Loan Company, the additional $5 000 over and above his previous mortgage would have been paid to Sam Shark to reduce his mortgage.

Before leaving the subject of prepayment privileges, it should be noted that the Canada Interest Act provides that any mortgage taken out by an individual (as opposed to a corporation) can, despite its wording, be prepaid after five years upon payment of the outstanding balance plus an additional three months' interest as a penalty.

d. MISCELLANEOUS INFORMATION ABOUT MORTGAGES

1. Priorities

Basically, a first mortgage is a first charge against the property mortgaged for the amount owing under the mortgage. A second mortgage is a second charge against the property mortgaged for the amount owing, and so on. Therefore, if a borrower runs into difficulties, the first mortgage would be entitled to be paid out first, the second mortgage to be paid out second, and so on.

A person can obtain as many mortgages against property as investors can be found who are willing to lend money against the security of such property. Therefore, it stands to reason that, usually, the more mortgages that are registered against the property, the higher the interest rate is on each successive mortgage, because the risk of non-payment increases with the number of mortgages registered. If, for example, a person had four mortgages registered against a piece of property, the interest rate on the fourth mortgage would likely be the highest since, in a clutch situation, it is the one with the least security behind it.

2. Discharges

When a mortgage is paid out, it is imperative that the borrower obtain from the lender a Discharge of Mortgage in registrable form and that it be registered immediately in the appropriate Land Title Office.

It is not enough to merely repay the money and feel relieved that the burden is gone. In the event of a sale or remortgage, the true status of the title must be known and reflected in the Land Title Office. The cost to the borrower of having a lawyer discharge a mortgage is currently between $60 and $90, although in some instances the lender, if requested, will provide it free of charge. However, if the mortgage discharge is not requested until later, when the lender has died or disappeared, the cost could run many times the standard cost, depending on the severity of the problems encountered.

3. Amortization schedules and payments

It stands to reason that, in order to avoid disputes between the lender and the borrower as to the amount outstanding at any time under the mortgage, both parties should keep proper records. This would include keeping an accurate list of payment dates and amounts, together with supporting records such as cancelled cheques, receipts, and deposit slips or books.

If there is a dispute, the onus of proving that a mortgage has been repaid in full lies with the borrower. Many private individuals lodge their mortgages or agreements with banks which will, for a nominal service charge, calculate and keep track of the payments received and the balance outstanding. Many computer companies will also, if they are given certain facts, provide computer print-outs of mortgage amortization schedules, of course basing them on the assumption that payments will be made on time. This is probably one of the best ways of knowing the status at all times. You can locate services like this by looking in the Yellow Pages under "data processing service."

If you want such a schedule, be sure to ask your lawyer at the time the mortgage is being arranged.

111

4. Interest compounding

Interest can be calculated in many ways. When interest is calculated separately and kept separate for one year before being added back to the principal for the purposes of the interest calculations for the following year, the mortgage is being compounded annually.

When interest payments are being calculated separately and added back to the principal for future interest calculations every six months, the mortgage is being compounded semi-annually.

When interest calculations are being done monthly and the accumulated interest added back to the principal for interest calculation purposes for the next month, the mortgage is being compounded monthly. It stands to reason that the more often the mortgage is compounded, the higher the effective interest rate will be.

The Canada Interest Act states that the rate of interest on mortgages should be stated in either annual compounding or semi-annual compounding rates. Consequently, most conventional lenders compound their mortgages semi-annually.

It is interesting to note that most credit unions in British Columbia calculate their interest on the reducing balance outstanding and, therefore, compound their mortgages monthly. This produces a higher effective rate of interest. A conventional lender advertising rates at 12% per annum compounded semi-annually would only have to disclose 12% in the Canada Interest Statement contained in the mortgage. The equivalent rate for a lender also advertising mortgage monies at 12% but compounding monthly is 12.30403% compounded semi-annually and should be disclosed in that manner in the Canada Interest Statement in the mortgage.

For the benefit of private individuals who are doing their own mortgage calculation, it should be noted that calculating the interest at the rate given in the mortgage on a monthly basis and subtracting this figure from the payment and treating the balance as principal to be applied in reduction of the mortgage results in monthly compounding and is, therefore, incorrect if the interest under the mortgage is compounded or calculated semi-annually.

5. Life insurance and mortgage debts

Most mortgages taken out today are substantial monetary obligations. If the principal wage earner should die suddenly, the burden of repaying the mortgage would, in most instances, pass to the home owner's family, who can probably least afford it. Such a burden to the family could be substantially lessened if the home owner had life insurance which would, at the home owner's death, be sufficient to repay the mortgage.

One of the cheapest types of life insurance that a home owner can obtain to cover this situation is known as "reducing term insurance." The coverage under such an insurance plan reduces as time progresses in much the same way as the principal balance outstanding under a mortgage reduces.

Insurance, of course, should fit the individual's situation. If you are interested in obtaining this type of protection, contact a life insurance agent specializing in "term" insurance. Do not buy any life insurance other than reducing term or possibly straight term if you want the most protection for the least cost. Also, shop around, as rates vary greatly.

6. Assumption or assignment of a mortgage

Many lenders provide, for obvious reasons, that their mortgage cannot be assumed by a third party unless they consent to such an assumption. Therefore, a property owner selling a property "cash to assumption of mortgage," should first make sure that this can, in fact, be done by checking the mortgage document for any clauses which prohibit such assumption.

In most mortgages, the lender's interest in the mortgage can be assigned to a third party unless there are any provisions in the mortgage restricting such a transfer.

Thus, for example, if the lender, instead of receiving monthly payments, wanted to be paid out and the borrower was not in a position to do so, the lender could sell and assign the debt to a third party. In return for such sale and assignment, the old lender would receive a lump sum payment. This payment, however, does not necessarily equal the amount that is outstanding under the mortgage. Depending upon the terms of the mortgage and the current interest rates available, the lender may be able to do one of the following:

(a) Sell the mortgage at par (i.e., for the amount outstanding under the mortgage)

(b) Sell at a premium (i.e., for more than the amount that is outstanding under the mortgage)

(c) Sell at a discount (i.e., for less than the amount that is outstanding under the mortgage)

An example of selling at a discount is when $10 000 is outstanding under a mortgage that provides for interest at 10% with a maturity date one year hence and no payments until then. One year hence the lender will receive a total payment of $11 000 from the borrower.

If the purchaser of the mortgage paid only $9 000 for the mortgage, the $9 000 payment would entitle the purchaser to receive $11 000 one year hence and the investment would yield $2 000 on the $9 000 invested for a total return in excess of 22% as compared to the previous 10%.

To obtain any benefits that may become available as a result of the lender's wishing to sell his or her interest, a borrower could request and usually would obtain from a private lender a right to first refusal on the sale by the lender of the mortgage. This gives the borrower an opportunity to cash out the mortgage at perhaps less than what is actually owing.

When a lender wishes to sell a mortgage, the purchaser should make sure that a proper registrable assignment is given and such assignment registered in the Land Title Office. Not only should notice of the assignment be given in writing by the assignee (i.e., old lender and seller) to the borrower, but to further protect the purchaser, a statement confirming the balance outstanding under the mortgage should be obtained from the borrower.

If the property is sold and the mortgage is assumed by a new purchaser, this person should agree to assume all liability and to protect the original borrower from any possible claims. It must be remembered that the mortgage document is a contract between the original borrower and the mortgagee and, if the person assuming the mortgage defaults under the mortgage, the original borrower can still be held liable on a *personal covenant*. If this happens, get professional assistance immediately.

7. Discounting: beware!

Many lenders, particularly in the secondary financing field, prefer to "write mortgages at a discount." The word "discount" implies savings. The savings, however, are made by the lender *not* by the borrower. When arranging secondary financing from private lenders and small mortgage companies, you cannot be too careful.

Consider the situation of one of Sam Shark's other "clients," Sue Sucker. Sue needed $4 000 to cover various personal expenses that she had suddenly incurred. Sue believed that during the year she would be able to save enough money to repay the whole loan after one year. She had an equity of $10 000 in her home. Sam was more than happy to lend her $4 000 and they agreed on a rate of interest at 18% per annum after Sam had convinced her that that was the going rate for second mortgages.

Sam then informed her that he did not have the money himself but had an investor who would be putting up the money and that he would assign the mortgage over to his investor. But, as no one can work for nothing and as it was the investor who would get the 18%, it would only be fair if he were paid for his work for finding the money that she so desperately needed.

He convincingly insisted that he was not as greedy as the department store or hardware store which normally has a 50% mark-up on most items and that he was prepared to receive only 20%. Furthermore, since she needed the money, she would not have to pay his fee until next year when she would repay the mortgage principal. Just so that they both had something in writing, he would merely add his fee on to the mortgage amount.

This all seemed very reasonable to Sue Sucker and she consequently signed the mortgage for $5 000 carrying interest at 18% for the one-year term. Sam Shark advanced her $4 000, immediately sold the mortgage to his investor for $5 000 and, pocketing the difference, went on to his next client. Sam had received 20% of the $5 000 as his fee and his investor received 18% on the amount that he had invested. But, Sue Sucker, in addition to repaying her loan of $4 000 would, at the end of one year, have to pay $900 in interest plus an additional $1 000 more than she had borrowed for a total cost to her of $1 900 in one year. *This is equivalent to 47.5% per annum.*

8. Consumer protection

Such discounting has been the subject of controversy in the last couple of years and some legislation is available to protect the borrower from unconscionable lenders. The Small Loans Act is a federal statute that specifies a maximum interest rate that may be charged. It governs, however, loans for amounts of only $1 500 or less.

The courts have interpreted that the $1 500 figure as set out in the act excludes bonuses. Therefore, a mortgage securing the sum of $2 000, of which $600 is a bonus, would not come under the jurisdiction of the Small Loans Act, even though the amount actually received by the borrower was only $1 400. This is the reason most loan companies do not advertise loans of under $1 500. They are not interested in lending sums below that figure, since the interest rates are controlled.

The Consumer Protection Act does not stipulate what is or is not a fair cost of borrowing. The act does, however, provide that, where the cost of borrowing money is excessive, harsh, or unconscionable, a judge may review the transaction and set it aside, alter it, or revise it. This becomes somewhat more difficult, however, where a mortgage has been assigned to a third party who was not aware of the previous history of the mortgage and has purchased it in good faith.

Perhaps the best protection that a borrower has is the Mortgage Brokers Act. This act requires that the lender, if lending money on a mortgage where the borrower is required to pay a bonus, commission, discount, finder's fee, brokerage fee, or an amount of a similar kind in addition to interest, must give the borrower a full disclosure statement setting out all costs and charges (see Sample #7).

The borrower is also given 48 hours to cancel the loan after signing the disclosure statement and can do this by delivering a copy of the disclosure statement to the appropriate Land Title Office, giving the registrar notice of the cancellation in a letter, and repaying the amount advanced.

A mortgage broker in the act is defined as a person who falls into one of the following classifications:

(a) One who carries on a business of lending money secured by mortgages (whether it is the broker's own money or that of others)

(b) One who is held out as such

(c) One who buys and sells mortgages

117

MORTGAGE DISCLOSURE STATEMENT

DISCLOSURE STATEMENT (i)
(Pursuant to *Mortgage Brokers Act*)
Province of British Columbia

1. Principal amount of Mortgage is   FIVE THOUSAND DOLLARS $5 000.00

2. Deduct:

   (a) Bonus or discount paid by borrower $ Nil

   (b) Brokerage fees, commission, finders fee, or other costs $1 000.00

   (c) Inspection or appraisal costs (ii) $ Nil

   (d) Estimated survey costs (iii) $ Nil

   (e) Estimated legal fees and disbursements $125.00

   Total deductions $ 1 125.00   1 125.00

3. Total amount to be paid to the borrower or for his/her account
   (difference between items 1 and 2) $ 3 875.00 (iv)

4. The effective annual rate of interest to be paid by the borrower is   47.5 % (v)

5. The amount and frequency of instalment payments will be $ 75.00 payable monthly .

6. Will the mortgage fall due at the option of the lender if the property is sold?
   Yes ☒   No ☐

7. The mortgage will become due and payable on the __1st__ day of __April__ , 199-
   at which time the borrower will owe not more than $ 5 000.00 .   (vi)

8. There is no right to renew this mortgage on the same terms when it falls due.

9. This mortgage may be paid off by the borrower after__ one (1) month __
   upon payment of the balance then owing and (if applicable)__ Nil __months' interest.

10. The street address is__ 27 "A" Water Way __
    and the legal description of the mortgaged property is:

    Lot Thirteen (13) of the
    South half (S½) of
    Block Fourteen (14)
    District Lot Fifteen (15)
    Plan 16
    New Westminster District

    I/We, SAM SHARK __ of __ 123 Thistle Path, Vancouver __
    (Name)   *(Address)*

the (agent of the) lender in this mortgage, have fully completed the above statement in triplicate.

Sam Shark
_____
Signature of lender or agent

I/We, SUE SUCKER __ of __ 27 "A" Water Way __
(Name(s))   *(Address(es))*

The borrower in this mortgage, acknowledge receipt of the above statement which I/we received
on the __29th__ day of __March__ , 199- at __10:00__ a.m./p.m.

_____   *Sue Sucker*
Signature of borrower   _____
                                        Signature of borrower

SAMPLE #7 — Continued

BORROWER'S RIGHT TO CANCEL

Under Section 16 of the *Mortgage Brokers Act,* where the lender furnishes a disclosure statement such as this, the borrower may cancel or rescind the mortgage within 48 hours after he/she signs the mortgage or receives the statement, whichever first occurs.

To be effective, Notice of Rescission in the form below must be given by delivering or posting by PREPAID mail to BOTH the lender and the appropriate Registrar of Titles (whose address appears below) within 48 hours, but Saturdays, Sundays, or holidays are not included in the calculation of time. Notice is effective at the time of mailing.

Borrowers will receive three copies of this form. Notice of Rescission should be given by sending one copy of THIS WHOLE FORM containing a signed copy of the Notice of Rescission to the lender and another signed copy to the appropriate Registrar of Titles. The borrower should keep the third copy.

A borrower who gives Notice of Rescission is required to forthwith repay to the lender all amounts he/she has actually received under the mortgage and interest plus the expenses reasonably and necessarily incurred by the lender. In return the lender is required to furnish a discharge of the mortgage. In the event of a dispute either party may apply to the Court.

In addition to the right to rescind, a borrower who has been deliberately misled by anything contained in this disclosure statement may apply to the Court within one month after signing the mortgage, to redeem the mortgaged property and to obtain an order that the mortgage be discharged upon payment into Court of the full amount actually advanced under the mortgage and interest plus the expenses reasonably and necessarily incurred by the lender.

There may be additional remedies available to the borrower under Part IV of the *Consumer Protection Act.*

MORTGAGE BROKERS ACT
(Section 16)
BORROWER'S NOTICE OF RESCISSION

To: THE REGISTRAR OF TITLES   To:_____

      LAND REGISTRY OFFICE   *(Name of lender)*

      _____, B.C.   _____

                                                   (Address)

....

Pursuant to Section 16 of the *Mortgage Brokers Act,* I rescind the mortgage described on the reverse side hereof.

My address for service of notices is _____

Dated at _____, B.C. this _____ day of _____, 199__

                                   _____

                                   (Signature of borrower)

NOTE — You should have been given three copies of this form. If you intend to use the Notice of Rescission, send one copy of this whole form containing a signed copy of the Notice of Rescission to the appropriate Registrar of Titles and another signed copy to the lender. Retain the third copy for yourself.

(d) One who receives yearly more than $1 000 in fees or other consideration for arranging mortgages

(e) One who lends money on more than 10 mortgages

A mortgage broker must also be registered with the government. Insurance companies, banks, credit unions, or trust companies are exempt.

9. Mortgaging a mortgage

Before leaving the general subject of mortgages, it should be mentioned that it is possible to mortgage a mortgage. For instance, a lender holding a mortgage of, for example, $25 000, and wishing to raise some cash, does not necessarily have to sell and assign the mortgage as previously discussed. Instead, the lender could find an investor who would be prepared to lend money with the mortgage as the security. This security would be a mortgage of the mortgage, and the lender of the mortgage being mortgaged would make repayment arrangements with the investor. A vendor's interest in an agreement for sale can likewise be mortgaged.

e. THE AGREEMENT FOR SALE

The agreement for sale is basically a charge that can be registered against the property being sold. The agreement for sale contains all the conditions of the purchase, such as the amount the property was purchased for, the amount that was paid down, the amount and dates of payment of the outstanding money, the interest rate, the due date, and the vendor's remedies in the event that the purchaser does not abide by the agreement.

As mentioned previously, the agreement for sale is a charge that the purchaser can register against the title until the payments under the agreement have been completed, at which time title is then transferred into the purchaser's name.

This is in contrast to the situation where the purchaser obtains title to the property and then mortgages that title by allowing the mortgage company to register a charge against it. Making sure that title is transferred when the agreement is paid off is as important as registering the discharge of mortgage previously discussed.

Although the basic principle is the same behind both the agreement and the mortgage, there are slight differences. The normal agreement for sale usually allows the purchaser to prepay the balance outstanding at any time without notice, penalty, or bonus — in contrast to the conventional mortgage. In addition, the standard redemption period if the agreement went to foreclosure (see chapter 10 on foreclosure) is three months for an agreement for sale and six months for the standard mortgage.

Also, since title is not being transferred, the purchaser's legal fees are initially smaller than if the purchase had been made by law of transfer of title and mortgage back to the vendor. However, the purchaser will probably eventually want to obtain title to the property and, in order to do so, would incur further legal fees. The total of these legal fees would, in all likelihood, be greater than if the title had been transferred initially.

The agreement for sale is somewhat of a peculiarity to British Columbia law, and the law relating to it is not as well settled as that relating to mortgage law. Because of this, many federal statutes, such as the Interest Act, do not apply to agreements for sale. This is the reason that no interest disclosure for the purpose of the Canada Interest Act is required in the agreement for sale. The Consumer Protection Act, however, does apply.

The general clauses contained in the standard mortgage (as previously discussed) are also usually contained in the agreement for sale or "Right to Purchase" as it is also sometimes called.

f. CONDITIONAL SALES CONTRACT AND CHATTEL MORTGAGES

You will recall our earlier discussion of two types of property: real property and personal property. Real property includes land and everything permanently attached to it, such as buildings, swimming pools, and fixtures in the buildings. Personal property or chattels are movable property. Chattels can also be mortgaged. This is done by way of a security agreement under the Personal Property Security Act. Just as mortgages are registered in the Land Title Office, security agreements can be registered with the Registrar General in Victoria to give the lender or vendor protection.

However, in instances where the "thing" being purchased is an item that benefits the owner of the land, such as a new furnace, hot water heater, or even a mobile home, the vendor is also able to register a notice of the security agreement on the title to the property in order to provide further security for payment.

It is possible that the vendor of the item may register such a notice of security agreement without the property owner having any knowledge of its registration until, perhaps, the property is sold, which could be several years after the last payment was made to the vendor.

Therefore, a property owner who purchases major articles, such as a furnace, hot water heater, or mobile home, and signs a security agreement should find out if the vendor will be registering a notice of the security agreement on the title to the property.

If so, the property owner should make sure that a release of the notice of the security agreement is obtained when the final payment is made under the contract.

6

TYPES OF FINANCING AVAILABLE IN B.C. AND WHERE TO FIND THEM

a. HOW WELL OFF ARE YOU FINANCIALLY?

Before we discuss financing in detail, remember to refer again to chapter 1 and particularly to the income requirements to support the financing. Unless these income requirements are met, many mortgage companies will not consider the mortgage application.

In quick review, the general rule followed by most conventional mortgage lenders is that borrowers should not commit themselves to more than 27% to 30% or at the outside, 33% of their gross salary for their monthly mortgage payments, including taxes.

Thus, if gross monthly income is $3 000,

27% is $810

30% is $900

33% is $990

Therefore, a person with an income of $3 000 per month before deductions should normally not pay more than $810 to $990 per month on combined mortgages (including taxes).

Of course, there are other factors that a lender will examine to determine what gross debt servicing ratio a borrower can afford. Some of these are other debts, availability of other income, family size, credit rating, the stage of a person's career, and the spouse's income. Some companies will allow all of a wife's income to be included with the husband's salary, while others will allow only part or none. Most lenders will now recognize 100% of both spouses' salaries for this calculation.

Once you know the monthly payment you can afford, the size of mortgage you can handle is easy to calculate. Assume you can afford a $900 monthly payment and net (after allowing for the home-owner grant) taxes are $1 200 per year. Then:

Monthly payment $900

Minus monthly taxes owed
    ($\frac{1}{12}$th of $1 200)   100

Amount available for principal
    and interest $800

To calculate the principal amount of mortgage that you can get for $800 per month, look at Table #1. It shows the monthly payments required to repay a loan of $1 000 at a given interest rate over a period of 15, 20, or 25 years. From that table you can see that with an interest rate of 12% per annum, a monthly payment of $10.32 would repay $1 000 in 25 years, whereas it would require $10.81 to repay the same amount in 20 years, or $11.82 a month over a 15-year period. Therefore, assuming that you could obtain a mortgage at 12% interest on a 25-year repayment plan (25-year amortization is standard on conventional mortgages), the sum of $800 per month would handle a mortgage of:

$$\frac{\$800 \times \$1\ 000}{\$10.32} = \$77\ 519$$

However, if you were able to obtain a mortgage at 10% interest instead, the same monthly payment of $800 per month would handle a mortgage of:

$$\frac{\$800 \times \$1\ 000}{\$8.95} = \$89\ 385$$

or a mortgage of $11 866 more for the same payment!

Table #2 shows what your minimum monthly income should be to pay some typical monthly mortgage payments.

Many lenders will now pre-approve applicants for a mortgage. This allows you to know exactly how much of a mortgage you can obtain, subject only to an appraisal of the property you purchase. Therefore, if you have $25 000 and can qualify for a mortgage of $175 000, you can spend $200 000 on a property. Please note that if, as in this example, the mortgage ($175 000) exceeds 75% of the purchase price ($200 000) the mortgage will be considered a "high ratio" mortgage (see section **d.** below).

b. COSTS

The cost of obtaining a mortgage should also be considered by a borrower. The cost will vary from lender to lender and depends on what type of financing is obtained. Some of the most common charges are for the following items.

1. Legal

Since the lenders are lending the funds, they want to make sure that their mortgage documentation is correct and that the security has been registered properly. They, therefore, want to select and use their own legal counsel, and the borrowers end up paying for the lenders' lawyers.

This is standard practice in the industry and the fees include not only the legal fees but also the disbursements that have been incurred in connection with drawing and registering the mortgage.

The standard practice is for these funds to be deducted directly from the money advanced under the mortgage. The amount of such fees can be ascertained by asking the lawyer handling the mortgage documentation, but they should be about the same as those in chapter 9.

TABLE #1
MONTHLY PRINCIPAL AND INTEREST PAYMENTS REQUIRED TO PAY $1 000*
FOR THE AMORTIZATION PERIOD INDICATED

Interest rate (%)	Amortization Period Years					
	10	15	20	25	30	35
6	$11.07	8.40	7.13	6.40	5.95	5.66
6¼	11.19	8.54	7.27	6.55	6.11	5.82
6½	11.32	8.67	7.41	6.70	6.27	5.99
6¾	11.44	8.80	7.55	6.86	6.43	6.15
7	11.56	8.94	7.70	7.01	6.59	6.32
7¼	11.69	9.07	7.84	7.16	6.75	6.49
7½	11.82	9.21	7.99	7.32	6.92	6.67
7¾	11.94	9.35	8.14	7.48	7.08	6.84
8	12.07	9.49	8.29	7.64	7.25	7.01
8¼	12.20	9.63	8.44	7.80	7.42	7.19
8½	12.33	9.77	8.59	7.96	7.59	7.37
8¾	12.45	9.91	8.74	8.12	7.76	7.54
9	12.58	10.05	8.90	8.28	7.93	7.72
9¼	12.71	10.19	9.05	8.45	8.11	7.90
9½	12.84	10.34	9.21	8.62	8.28	8.08
9¾	12.98	10.48	9.36	8.78	8.46	8.26
10	13.10	10.62	9.52	8.94	8.63	8.44
10¼	13.24	10.77	9.68	9.11	8.80	8.63
10½	13.37	10.92	9.83	9.28	8.99	8.80
10¾	13.50	11.06	10.00	9.45	9.16	8.99
11	13.64	11.21	10.16	9.63	9.34	9.18
11¼	13.77	11.36	10.32	9.80	9.52	9.37
11½	13.91	11.51	10.48	9.97	9.70	9.55
11¾	14.04	11.66	10.65	10.14	9.88	9.74
12	14.18	11.82	10.81	10.32	10.06	9.93
12¼	14.32	11.97	10.98	10.49	10.25	10.11
12½	14.46	12.12	11.14	10.67	10.43	10.30
12¾	14.59	12.28	11.31	10.85	10.61	10.49
13	14.74	12.44	11.48	11.03	10.80	10.69
13¼	14.88	12.59	11.65	11.21	10.99	10.88
13½	15.02	12.75	11.82	11.39	11.17	11.07
13¾	15.16	12.90	11.99	11.56	11.36	11.26
14	15.30	13.06	12.16	11.74	11.54	11.45
14¼	15.44	13.22	12.33	11.92	11.73	11.64
14½	15.58	13.38	12.50	12.10	11.92	11.83
14¾	15.72	13.54	12.67	12.29	12.10	12.02
15	15.87	13.70	12.84	12.47	12.29	12.21
15¼	16.01	13.86	13.02	12.65	12.48	12.40
15½	16.15	14.02	13.19	12.83	12.67	12.59
15¾	16.30	14.18	13.36	13.01	12.86	12.78

*Based on interest compounded semi-annually.

TABLE #2
MONTHLY SALARY REQUIRED
FOR MORTGAGE PAYMENTS

Monthly mortgage payment including taxes	Monthly salary required based on gross debt service ratio of:		
	27%	30%	33%
$150	$ 555	$ 500	$ 455
300	1111	1000	909
450	1666	1500	1364
600	2222	2000	1818
750	2778	2500	2273
900	3333	3000	2727
1050	3889	3500	3182
1200	4444	4000	3636
1350	5000	4500	4091
1500	5556	5000	4545
1650	6111	5500	5000
1800	6667	6000	5455

2. Survey

The survey certificate has already been discussed in some detail in chapter 3. A survey certificate is usually required by the conventional mortgage lender.

The cost of obtaining the survey at the time of writing is approximately $150 to $200 for the ordinary home.

Again, the cost of the certificate is charged against the borrower, and, unless the fee has been prepaid, will be deducted from the amount advanced under the mortgage.

3. Tax adjustment

Mortgage companies and financial institutions deal with taxes primarily in two ways. They require that the borrower either pay the taxes as they become due or pay one-twelfth of the estimated annual taxes each month, in addition to the mortgage payment.

The companies that collect tax payments monthly handle these payments in different ways. Some mortgage companies will put them into a separate tax account on which they pay interest as the tax payments accumulate, while other mortgage companies do not pay any interest on their tax accounts.

Still other mortgage companies take the payments and apply them against principal and interest. When the taxes become due, they pay the balance owing, and the amount of these taxes is then added to the then outstanding principal. On the whole, this method is probably the best for the borrower.

For the mortgage companies that run a separate tax account, a problem occurs when the mortgage is obtained at a time when there is less than one year left before the property taxes become due. For example, if taxes are due six months after the mortgage has been taken out, the mortgage company, by collecting one-twelfth of the taxes each month, will obviously not have sufficient funds on hand to pay the taxes when they become due.

Some mortgage companies will bill the borrower separately for the difference as soon as the tax figures are available, while other mortgage companies will estimate the adjustments at the time the mortgage is taken out and deduct the funds from the proceeds thus producing a smaller advance. Please note that this is a prepayment of expenses rather than an additional cost.

The borrower should attempt to determine what the situation is with the lender and make adjustments accordingly. Please also note that the lender will want to ensure that the current year's taxes are paid and, again, if they are not, the company will deduct the amount from the proceeds and pay them on behalf of the borrower.

4.   Interest adjustment

A number of lending institutions will also make an interest adjustment and deduct such amount from the net advance of the mortgage. This again is a prepayment of expenses rather than an additional cost. The interest adjustment is the amount of interest that accumulates from the date the funds are advanced up to the date one month preceding the date the first mortgage payment is made.

Assume for the purposes of illustration that the advance of funds was made on January 23 and that mortgage payments are to be made on the first day of every month. The interest adjustment is equal to the interest calculated on the principal of the mortgage advanced from January 23 to February 1.

This interest adjustment is then deducted from the money advanced on January 23 so that the interest is prepaid up to February 1. The first payment date, therefore, becomes March 1, at which time the normal mortgage payment will be made

129

covering one month's interest plus the repayment of a small amount of principal.

Again a borrower should determine whether an interest adjustment will be made at the time the funds are advanced; it will affect the net proceeds received under the mortgage.

5.   Fire insurance

The lender will require that the borrower carry fire insurance with loss payable first (for a first mortgage) to the first lender, second to the second lender, and so on. It is the borrower's responsibility to carry insurance for an amount sufficient to replace the home. The lender's lawyer will require proof of such insurance before money is advanced. Since the borrower, in most cases, makes the insurance arrangements, there will be no deduction from the mortgage proceeds. The cost of obtaining such insurance should, nevertheless, be considered.

6.   Appraisal fees

The lender, before considering loaning money against a property, will want to appoint an appraiser and have an appraisal done. This will show not only that there is value in the security, but also what the value is for the purposes of the mortgage ratios.

Again, it is customary that the cost of such appraisal be borne by the borrower. A standard appraisal for a standard home is around $150. This is usually paid out of the deposit left by the borrower with the lender at the time the mortgage application is made or else deducted from the proceeds of the mortgage.

7.   Credit reports

Some mortgage companies charge the borrower for the cost of obtaining credit reports and other such information. These charges are usually relatively minor (approximately $15).

8. Stand-by fees

Some mortgage institutions will attempt to charge a stand-by fee to the borrower. The justification for such a fee is that it is reimbursement for loss of revenue on money set aside and reserved for the borrower until it is advanced. This isn't a common charge and should be avoided if possible.

9. Processing fees

Some mortgage companies will attempt to charge processing fees. The rationale behind the processing fee is that it is reimbursement to them for the administrative expenses incurred in processing the mortgage. This is in essence a double charge as that is what the interest is being paid for and, again, should be avoided. The processing fee and the stand-by fee are in reality only two ways of increasing the yield on the mortgage to the lender.

c. CONVENTIONAL MORTGAGES

The rule for a conventional first mortgage is that a person can borrow up to 75% of the value of the lot and the house. The borrower will thus have to supply at least 25% of the value to be able to borrow 75%.

The largest proportion of conventional loans are written by life insurance companies, trust companies, or chartered banks. Most of the funds of these companies used for these types of loans are governed by either federal or provincial statutes restricting the loans to the foregoing ratios and to the fact that such mortgages must be first mortgages.

The legislation does not prescribe a maximum loan amount, but many companies have a limit on house mortgages. These limits vary with the company, the area of property, and the economic times, but few companies like to exceed $250 000. These limits should be checked before any critical decisions are made. The mortgage interest rate varies from time to time and from institution to institution. However, although most institutions are usually fairly competitive, it does pay to check around.

Conventional mortgages are available on both new and existing houses. The mortgages are repaid in monthly installments which frequently include an amount for municipal taxes. The standard amortization period is 25 years. The most usual terms of a mortgage are 1, 2, 3, or 5 years. Very few, if any, lenders are still granting terms that correspond to the amortization period, usually 25 years, with the interest rate remaining constant during the repayment period.

In the instances of the five-year term or less, the lender, who does not need the funds or has not had problems with the mortgage, generally renews the mortgage at the expiration of the term for an additional term as may be negotiated at the then-current interest rate. If the lender refuses to renew, the borrower must repay the loan or obtain a new mortgage elsewhere.

d. HIGH RATIO MORTGAGE LOANS

Many conventional lenders are approved to provide high ratio mortgage loans. In high ratio loans, the lender will insure the mortgage against investment loss if the borrower defaults under the mortgage and the lender suffers a loss as a result.

Such insurance should not be confused with life insurance. It is not the borrower who insures against liability to the mortgage company, but the mortgage company that insures against loss in the event of default and loss under the mortgage. The best known mortgage insurance companies are the Mortgage Insurance Company of Canada (M.I.C.C.) and Canada Mortgage and Housing Corporation (CMHC).

Mortgage insurance enables the conventional lender to lend more than the conventional 75% of appraised value. M.I.C.C. and CMHC currently allow the following amount to be borrowed based on appraised value for single detached houses, duplexes, and condominiums that are purchased for owner occupation:

95% of the first $180 000

80% of the balance

On refinancings this changes to 85% of the first $125 000 and on non-owner-occupied, it is 85% of the first $185 000.

The insurer must approve the loan first. On 95% loans M.I.C.C. is very selective with respect to not only the quality of the property, but also the quality of the applicants. The maximum gross debt service (G.D.S.) for P.I.T. plus 50% of condominium fees cannot exceed 30% of income from employment (or 32% if energy costs are included) and no more than 40% for total debt service. Once the loan is approved, the insurer charges an insurance fee based on the face amount of the loan.

M.I.C.C.'s charges are as follows:

Loan to Value Ratio	Existing Housing
to 65%	0.5%
65% - 75%	0.75%
75% - 80%	1.25%
80% - 85%	2.0%
85% - 90%	2.5%

Add 0.5% for approved insured progress advances (i.e., more than one advance over 75%) or equity take-out refinancing loans.

This insurance fee is passed on to the borrower. The premium does not need to be paid in cash out of the borrower's own funds, but can be borrowed from the lender who then adds it to the mortgage and adjusts the payments accordingly, based on the amortization period. Thus, an 82%, $150 000 loan would be a $153 000 insured loan with corresponding slightly higher monthly payments. The additional

$3 000 would be the insurance fee and would be paid out of the mortgage advance, so that the advance under both mortgages would be equal.

In addition to the insurance fee, there is also an application fee of $75 to $235, which is usually paid by the borrower. The interest rate on a high ratio mortgage loan is usually equal to or only slightly above the rate for a 75% conventional mortgage. The repayment arrangements are the same as for the conventional mortgages and so are the requirements. In essence, only the mortgage has been insured. All other costs remain the same, as in the instance of the conventional mortgage.

The value of the insured mortgage is that it enables someone to purchase a house with a minimum down payment. For example, if the house value is $200 000, a borrower could obtain only $150 000 under a conventional mortgage and would thus require a down payment of $50 000. If the mortgage is insured, the borrower could, instead, obtain a mortgage of $187 000 (plus the premium) and would thus require a down payment of only $13 000.

e. FEDERAL GOVERNMENT ASSISTANCE

1. General

Federal government assistance is made available through the National Housing Act (N.H.A.). This act is administered by the Canada Mortgage and Housing Corporation (CMHC), the federal housing agency. In addition to concerning itself with mortgages and financial assistance for mortgages, it is involved in a number of other matters, such as housing research; urban planning and renewal; development of a market for mortgages; improved housing, design, and construction; and the provision of accommodation to meet the needs of special groups such as elderly persons, families, individuals with low incomes, and students. This section, however, deals primarily with the financial assistance programs that are available for home owners through CMHC.

2. N.H.A. mortgages

The National Housing Act authorized CMHC to insure loans to prospective home owners or to builders for new and existing housing. Such loans are usually not obtained from CMHC itself but from approved lenders, such as banks, life insurance companies, and trust and loan companies authorized by the federal government to lend under the terms of the National Housing Act.

A list of such companies can be obtained from the nearest office of CMHC. The loan is usually repaid on a 25-year amortization, but the repayment period can be shorter or longer if required. The interest rate is set by the lender.

To meet CMHC requirements, the borrowers must not spend more than 32% of their gross income toward payment of principal, interest, and taxes plus 50% of any condominium fees. The loan must also comply with their loan-to-lending ratios.

These insured loans are discussed in more detail in the previous section, although they do not necessarily need to be high ratio mortgage loans.

The one-time insurance premiums and loan limits are the same as those for the M.I.C.C. given above.

There is no maximum loan amount but to qualify for the mortgages you require at least 10% equity. The minimum term is one year and the amortization period can be up to 40 years. The mortgage document itself is a standard form approved by CMHC.

CMHC also has a special program for first-time homebuyers allowing them a maximum mortgage loan of 95% of the lending value of the home. In the Greater Vancouver area, the maximum house price that qualifies is $250 000. In expensive centres outside that area, the limit is $175 000. The limit drops to $125 000 elsewhere. The minimum mortgage term is five years.

For the buyer to qualify, the home must be occupied as a principal residence and at least one of the buyers (or the buyer, if only one) cannot have owned a home during the last five years. The buyers must also be able to meet payments for principal, interest, and property taxes plus 50% of condominium fees, if applicable, without spending more than 35% of their gross family income. Payments on their total debt load can not exceed 42% of gross family income. The insurance fee is 2.5% of the loan amount for a single advance and 3% of the loan amount for multiple advances.

Like most conventional mortgages, the insured mortgages are renewable at prevailing interest rates at intervals specified in the mortgage agreements without payment of a further insurance fee.

Construction of a new house for which a N.H.A. loan is required should not be started unless the loan has first been approved. It is essential that the builder first contact CMHC to become familiar with the current requirements and inspection procedure. Failure to do so could disqualify the home for insurance.

Once approved, the loan will be advanced in various installments as the house reaches various stages of construction. The amount of each advance is based on the percentage of work completed.

When advances are made during construction, the general practice is for the lender to ensure that the borrower's funds are invested first so that there is always a sufficient amount of the loan being held back to complete the house.

While the house is being built, CMHC will make a number of inspections of the construction. These are not full architectural or engineering inspections but are made to protect the investment of the lender by ensuring that the house is being built in a reasonable conformity to plans and specifications and the housing standards prescribed by CMHC. They also serve to check construction progress for the purpose of loan advances.

3. Other federal assistance

Other federal programs are also available to assist in providing better and more affordable housing. Only the more relevant programs are dealt with here in any detail; a brief mention is made of others.

Loans and, in some cases, subsidies for lower income tenants are available for rental housing to assist in the financing of the construction, purchase, or improvement of rental housing developments and even for the conversion of non-residential buildings to housing use. This type of assistance is provided through N.H.A.-insured mortgages for loans of up to 80% of the cost of the project as determined by CMHC. The minimum equity requirement is 20% and the minimum term is five years.

In addition, loans or subsidies are available to:

(a) Continuing Housing Co-operatives (an organization with a fairly large number of members organized for the collective ownership and management of some form of housing)

(b) Private non-profit housing corporations (where no part of the income is payable or available to the benefit of a proprietor, member, or shareholder)

(c) Public non-profit housing corporations (sponsored by a province or municipality)

(d) Rural and native housing committees under the Rural Native Housing Program. This program has two main objectives:

    (i) To provide better housing for families in rural Canada at prices and monthly payments they can afford

137

      (ii) To give eligible families in communities the opportunity to become involved in the entire housing process

In addition, the National Housing Act provides authority for chartered banks or other approved lenders to make loans for home improvements. These loans are again guaranteed by CMHC in return for an insurance fee equal to 1% of the amount of the loan.

The maximum loan is $10 000 for each family housing unit, unless you live in a rural area, in which case it is $25 000. The loan is normally secured by a promissory note. However, loans in excess of $10 000 must be secured by a mortgage. The loan is repayable in monthly installments amortized over not more than 25 years at the current market level.

Home improvement loans under the Residential Rehabilitation Assistance Program (R.R.A.P.) may be used to cover a wide variety of permanent alterations, repairs, and additions to permanent residences including the common areas of condominiums.

To be eligible for R.R.A.P. assistance the dwelling must be substandard in at least one of six basic areas: structural soundness, fire safety, electrical, plumbing, heating, and/or accessibility to a disabled occupant. Priority is given to repairs in these six basic areas, but various other improvements are permissible, including installation of insulation and other measures to improve thermal efficiency. The repairs should ensure a further useful life to the property of about 15 years.

The following categories are eligible for assistance:

(a) Home owners who meet property conditions and income criteria

(b) Landlords in selected municipalities who agree to rent control

(c) Non-profit corporations and cooperatives

(d) Indian band councils

(e) Home owners and landlords who are proposing to carry out renovations to make a unit more accessible to a disabled person

To qualify for a R.R.A.P. loan, the household income must be below established income ceilings which vary by household size and by area within the province. Part of the loan may be forgiven based on the following guidelines for a $10 000 loan:

Adjusted family income	Max. forgivable under normal circumstances	Max. forgivable when modifying dwelling for disabled access
$33 000 or more	$0	$0
31 000	0	1 000
29 000	0	2 000
27 000	0	3 000
25 000	0	4 000
23 000	0	5 000
21 000	1 000	5 000
19 000	2 000	5 000
17 000	3 000	5 000
15 000	4 000	5 000
13 000 or less	5 000	5 000

As the ground rules appear to be changing all the time and as new programs become available and old programs are withdrawn, it would be advisable for you to check with CMHC should any of the foregoing loan, assistance, or subsidy plans be of interest. Application forms can also be obtained from them. In Vancouver, CMHC is located at

#400 – 2600 Granville Street, Vancouver, B.C., V6H 3V7, (604) 731-5733.

f. PROVINCIAL GOVERNMENT ASSISTANCE

1. General

The provincial government also has assistance programs. The Home Purchase Assistance Act is designed to aid people in need of assistance. The program makes assistance available to the purchasers of new and older homes, provided the cost of the home is within specified price limits (to be discussed later).

Although the terms and types of assistance change from time to time, the only assistance available under this act at this time is a guarantee of up to $12 000 of the applicant's first, or under certain circumstances, second mortgage. At the time of writing the government's $10 000 second mortgage loan has been phased out.

2. The $12 000 mortgage loan guarantee

This mortgage loan guarantee is available for the purchase of one of the following:

(a) A new or older home that is a single-family dwelling

(b) A property that is subdivided under the Condominium Act

(c) A mobile home that is owned by the applicant and is affixed to the applicant's land or located in a mobile home park

The program, known as M.A.P., is designed to assist people who need extra help in buying a home. The provincial government guarantees up to $12 000 of the applicant's first, or sometimes second, mortgage. This allows an individual to borrow as much as 95% of the purchase price of the home and still qualify for mortgage insurance either with CMHC or

M.I.C.C. The applicant must, of course, be able to make payments on the debt in the usual way.

Under the M.A.P. program there is no government-issued second mortgage. The government guarantee is applied to a portion of the first or second mortgage from approved lending institutions such as banks, trust companies, and credit unions who then administer the mortgage entirely. The home buyer makes a single blended payment on the mortgage. M.A.P. borrowers will be permitted to transfer the first mortgage guarantee between approved lending institutions. This feature will permit the borrower to shop around for the best mortgage deal at renewal time.

The provincially guaranteed portion of the first mortgage cannot be greater than 50% of the mortgage, while in the case of a second mortgage, the province will guarantee the lesser of $12 000 or 100% of the second mortgage. The mortgage must be structured so that payments reduce the outstanding principal and mortgages that are payable on demand, interest only, re-advanceable, or provide for graduated payments are not acceptable. The home must not be on leased property and agreements for sale and conditional sales contracts do not qualify.

An applicant can assume an existing first mortgage with an M.A.P. guarantee already attached provided such applicant meets all the normal M.A.P. requirements. The home buyer can also assume an existing first mortgage without a guarantee attached and qualify for a provincial guarantee on the second mortgage. Please note, however, that an applicant cannot have a provincial guarantee on both the first and second mortgages.

The following criteria must be met in order to qualify for the M.A.P. guarantee.

(a) The cost of the home must be within the designated price limits in effect as of the date of purchase. This is currently $100 000 for all areas of the province.

(b) The home must be the mortgagor's principal place of residence and cannot be a holiday cottage, ski cabin, or other part-time home.

(c) The mortgagor must have a minimum down payment of $2 000 or 5% of the purchase price, whichever is greater.

(d) To be eligible a person cannot have received a grant or loan under the act previously. Even the spouse of a person who has received a grant or a loan previously is not eligible as long as they lived together in a residence. In short, it is a one-time help only.

(e) There are also residency requirements attached to the eligibility. Either you or your spouse, provided the spouse is registered on the title, must have —

- resided in British Columbia for a continuous period of not less than two years immediately prior to the purchase of the home,

- been born in British Columbia and be a Canadian citizen at the time of the application, or

- resided in British Columbia for a continuous period of five years at any time and be a Canadian citizen or permanent resident at the time of application.

If you have been an unsuccessful applicant but feel that special circumstances in your case should be considered, an eligibility committee established by the Minister will review your request.

Application forms and detailed instructions on how to apply can be obtained at the Loan Administration Branch, Ministry of Finance and Corporate Relations, 940 Blanshard Street, Victoria, B.C. V8N 3E6.

3. Concluding notes

The regulations, the programs, and the assistance available change regularly, and before relying on the information in this section, it is strongly recommended that you double-check with the appropriate government department to ensure that there has been no change.

g. CREDIT UNION FINANCING

In addition to the conventional lenders, credit union mortgage financing is also available. However, you have to be a member of a credit union before you can use their facilities and, among other things, apply for a mortgage loan; but in most instances, this is just a matter of making an application.

Credit unions are located throughout British Columbia and provide services to the members using them in that area. This is in sharp contrast to many of the conventional lenders, who prefer to restrict their mortgage loans to the metropolitan areas. In outlying areas, the credit unions are, therefore, probably some of the most important lenders.

Credit unions can be further contrasted to the conventional lenders in the following ways:

(a) Credit unions are, in most instances, much more flexible with their loan ratios. This should not be interpreted to mean that they make imprudent loans, but only that they are able to exercise more discretion with each application.

(b) Credit unions are prepared to accept unconventional security for their loans. They will take not only first mortgages, but also second mortgages, and mortgages of agreements for sale. The interest rate is usually fitted to the loan ratio rather than to the type of security. This could be of great benefit to the purchaser who wants to assume a low-interest mortgage or agreement for sale on the property that is being purchased, but who needs financing to come up with the remainder.

(c) Mortgages from credit unions can be life insured, so that if the borrower dies, the mortgage is automatically paid off. The insurance is group insurance, is very reasonable, and can be obtained without detailed medical checkups. (This is now also possible with conventional lenders.)

In comparison with the advantages that have just been listed, the disadvantages of a credit union mortgage are relatively minor:

(a) Credit union mortgages are not assumable, but must be paid out in full if the borrower's interest in the property is sold or otherwise transferred. Thus any new purchaser will either have to reapply to the credit union for financing or arrange financing elsewhere.

(b) The interest rates on most credit union mortgages are, as discussed in the previous chapter, compounded monthly instead of semi-annually, thus producing an effective interest rate slightly higher than the conventional lender although both could be quoting the same rate. However, some credit unions are now revising their procedure so that interest is charged on a semi-annual compounding basis the same as most conventional lenders.

Many of the conventional costs of obtaining a conventional mortgage, such as legal fees, interest adjustment, fire insurance, and appraisal fees are also applicable to obtaining a credit union mortgage. Normally, survey certificates, tax adjustments (credit unions normally do not require that taxes be paid with the mortgage payment), credit reports, stand-by fees, and processing fees are not required.

h. VENDOR FINANCING

This could be one of the best means of financing if it is available. The term "vendor financing" refers to the situation where the vendor (seller) of the property is prepared

144

to finance the purchase by leaving some of the equity in the property and allowing the purchaser to pay such equity over a period of time.

There are innumerable ways that a vendor can provide financing to the purchaser. It depends strictly on what the parties can work out between them and how much equity the vendor is prepared to leave behind.

The vendor, if looking for an income investment, may be prepared to grant a first mortgage to the purchaser or may be prepared to leave in only a smaller amount by way of a second or third mortgage. Alternatively, the vendor may be prepared to sell by way of an agreement for sale (see chapter 5, section **e.**).

The agreement for sale can be used as a "wrap around" for other mortgages, which can be advantageous to the vendor or the purchaser. The following examples illustrate the situations where such a "wrap around" could be used.

Our friends, Harry and Hilda Homeseeker, have found their dream home. They are trying to work something out with the owner, Ernie "Easy" Bucks. Ernie wants $126 000 for his home. The Homeseekers have decided that they can afford to spend only $120 000 maximum with a down payment of $20 000. Ernie has a $75 000 mortgage at 10% on his home. It becomes due in three years and would require a prepayment penalty if it was paid out earlier.

A compromise was reached whereby the Homeseekers agreed to purchase the home for $120 000, $20 000 down and the balance of $100 000 by way of agreement for sale at 12% per year with the agreement becoming due in three years on the due date of the mortgage.

The Homeseekers will make payments to Ernie who has agreed, under the agreement for sale, to make all payments to the mortgage company. The Homeseekers are happy as they have spent what they had budgeted for and no more, while our friend, Ernie "Easy" Bucks, was happy to sell at the reduced price, as he will more than make up the difference by charging 12% on $100 000 (approximately $12 000/year) under the agreement for sale while paying only 10% on $75 000 (approximately $7 500/year) of this money to the mortgage company and, furthermore, escaping the prepayment penalty.

A similar compromise situation could probably have been reached using the "wrap around" agreement for sale if, for instance, Ernie had been asking $126 000 for his home but had, in his own mind, been prepared to settle for $115 000. Now if Ernie had a $75 000 mortgage at 12% he, again, could have agreed to sell the property to the Homeseekers for $120 000 with $20 000 down and $100 000 by way of an agreement for sale carrying interest at 11%. The Homeseekers would again have obtained what they wanted and Ernie "Easy" Bucks would also have been satisfied.

Although he would have been responsible for the $75 000 mortgage and thus would have been borrowing $75 000 at 12% (interest cost of approximately $9 000/year) and lending that same money out at 11%, his total interest and monthly payments from the Homeseekers would have been based on $100 000 (interest cost of approximately $11 000/year) which would have been ample to cover his mortgage payment on the $75 000 and give him $5 000 more for his house than he had been prepared to settle for plus $2 000 interest income for a total return of $11 000 ($6 000 plus $5 000) over three years on his $25 000 equity left in the home. This would work out at an average annual return of 14.67%.

If you purchase under a "wrap around" agreement for sale and there is a mortgage that the vendor agrees to pay but doesn't, you can, as a lower ranking chargeholder on the title, be foreclosed. You should, for your protection, either advise the first mortgage company of the situation and ask them to notify you immediately if they don't get their payments, or provide in the agreement for sale that the payment on the first mortgage will be made directly to the mortgage company by you, and that the amount of the payment will be deducted from the payments due under the agreement for sale.

In this way, you can ensure that the mortgage payments are, in fact, made to the mortgage company and that you will not suddenly be involved in foreclosure proceedings even though you had fully complied with the terms under the agreement for sale.

As it is customary for the purchaser to always pay for the conveyancing when acquiring property, a purchaser is again responsible for the legal fees attributable to any mortgage given back to the vendor. These legal fees are paid to the purchaser's lawyer, who customarily draws the mortgage to the approval of the vendor.

Before leaving the subject of vendor financing, it should be pointed out that when a vendor is selling a home to a purchaser who intends to use the home as a residence and where "something has to give," there could be a considerable tax advantage if the vendor remained firm on the price but lowered the interest rate on the financing.

The money made on the sale of the "principal residence" would in all likelihood be tax free, whereas the money made on interest charges would be income and thus taxable.

i. SECONDARY FINANCING

The secondary financing field includes second and subsequent mortgages. As already discussed, the password to this field is "careful."

Secondary moneylenders range from a few respectable lenders to loan sharks. The one thing that they all have in common is that they are interested in a higher interest rate and/or yield than they can obtain on conventional first mortgages or on deposits elsewhere. The return on the interest rate is easily recognized. The effective yield, however, can be increased in numerous ways such as through discounts, grossed up appraisal allowances, stand-by fees, and processing fees.

Most of the fees discussed in the beginning of this chapter are applicable to this type of mortgage financing. The only exception is the tax adjustment, as it is not common for a secondary lender to collect taxes.

The best lenders are probably the banks if the money is required for a relatively short period of time and can be paid off during that time.

"Relatively short" means up to five years, although they will, in certain instances, go to ten years.

Credit unions provide some secondary financing at reasonable rates. Some trust companies have also entered the field. These alternatives are probably the least expensive in both rates and charges and should be tried first.

j. MORTGAGE FUNDS FROM YOUR OWN RRSP

Yes, that's right, you can now borrow money from yourself! Tax regulations now permit the owner of a self-directed RRSP to borrow mortgage funds for his or her own property from his or her own RRSP provided certain conditions are met, as follows:

(a) The mortgage must be secured by real estate in Canada

(b) The mortgage must be on terms generally available in the market

(c) The mortgage must be serviced by a lender approved under the National Housing Act (N.H.A.)

(d) The mortgage must be insured by a policy of mortgage insurance (e.g., M.I.C.C. or CMHC)

To meet the insurance requirement, the normal insurance fees previously discussed for these companies apply. You can mortgage your principal residence as well as that of your child. Your RRSP funds can also be used for second mortgages on these terms, or even loans on revenue properties. The latter case presents a particularly interesting situation as the interest paid will be an expense to you and, therefore, tax deductible, while the receipt of the interest by you in the RRSP will be tax free, at least until the RRSP is de-registered or the money is withdrawn.

7

ALTERNATIVE FORMS OF HOME OWNERSHIP

a. INTRODUCTION

As a result of a substantial demand for cheaper forms of housing, new types of home ownership have become popular, and this chapter discusses some of these forms — including condominiums (townhouses), cooperatives, lease lots, and trailer and mobile homes.

Condominiums and cooperatives are designed to maximize the use of common facilities including land and structural portions of the building, thereby creating savings for their owners. Lease lots have also become popular in the last few years as an attempt to keep the cost of the land portion of the home down, thus decreasing the overall cost of the home to the purchaser.

The savings on trailers and mobile homes can be attributed to two factors. First, the mobile home is cheaper to produce than the conventional house and, second, it does not necessarily involve a land purchase.

Many people think of condominium or cooperative ownership as ownership of an apartment or a townhouse. However, it is also possible to have condominium warehouses, office buildings, or even summer cottages. In fact, in Vancouver we have already seen the beginnings of condominium industrial structures. The words "condominium" and "cooperative" refer to legal structures, not physical structures. The legal structure of both condominiums and cooperatives allows subdivision of buildings, which permits some sort of individual ownership of part of the building.

In both condominiums and cooperatives, people are bound together by a corporation. Each member of the corporation has an exclusive right to use part of the property (a unit) and each member has a share of the remainder of the property (common property) in common with all of the other members. Each member, therefore, has an exclusive right and a shared right.

In cooperative ownership, a company is formed and this company is the owner of the entire property. The various members of the project own shares in this company (their shared right) and enter into a lease with the company for the specific dwelling unit that they occupy (their exclusive right).

As a shareholder of the company, an owner has a say in how the company is run and, thus, indirectly in how the project is run. A cooperative member who wishes to leave a suite must find someone to purchase the shares and take an assignment of the lease.

In a condominium project, the purchaser can obtain title in the Land Title Office to a particular dwelling unit (exclusive right) and become a co-owner with all the other members of the common property (shared right). As a co-owner, the purchaser also becomes a member of the strata corporation and, as such, has a say in the management of the project. Thus, it can be seen that, for condominiums, the owner receives a direct legal title to rights (both exclusive and shared), whereas in cooperatives, the owner receives these rights indirectly through a company.

The major difference between condominium ownership and cooperative ownership is a practical one and relates to mortgage and tax payments. In a cooperative project, since the company owns the property, there is only one mortgage and assessment to which each leaseholder must contribute. If

151

members default in their obligations to make mortgage or tax contributions, the other members must make up the default.

In the condominium situation, all members of the project have their own mortgage and tax assessments on their units. If one member of the project is in default, the remaining members are not required to remedy the default in mortgage or tax payments.

Condominium ownership is, and will in all likelihood continue to be, an increasingly important form of real estate ownership.

Cooperatives, which are more cumbersome, have been primarily used where condominium ownership has not been legally possible, but have now been somewhat curtailed by recent legislative changes. The major portion of this chapter is, therefore, about condominiums.

b. CONDOMINIUMS

1. Condominium Act

In 1966, when the Strata Titles Act was introduced in British Columbia, a new interest in land was created — the strata lot. This act was repealed and replaced by the Condominium Act in 1974.

Although there are many individual differences between the acts, the essence of both of them is that they allowed a building to be subdivided into two or more individual lots so that you could own a particular portion of any building in your own right and the common property jointly with others.

The physical and legal closeness of condominium ownership and the shared common property requires that there be certain rules and regulations to determine each owner's rights and obligations toward the other owners. These rules and regulations are contained in the Condominium Act itself and the bylaws of the strata corporation.

Both the strata lots, and the strata corporation, are automatically created when a strata plan ("subdivision plan") is filed in the Land Title Office. The members of the strata corporation are the owners of the strata lots for the time being. The strata corporation can be likened to a nonprofit company, society, or even a club. The Condominium Act and the bylaws can be viewed together as the constitution governing such a company, society, or club.

Some of the more important things that are dealt with in the Condominium Act are the creation, duties, and powers of the strata corporation, the voting rights of the members, the establishment and regulations governing the bylaws of the strata corporation, arbitration procedure for disputes between the strata corporation and an owner, regulations governing the rental of strata lots, and insurance on the buildings.

When the strata corporation is created, the Condominium Act provides that such a corporation automatically has the bylaws contained in that act. The bylaws are commonly referred to as the first and second schedules. In the case of a strata plan that is principally residential, these bylaws cannot be added to, amended, or repealed until after the first annual general meeting of the strata corporation or unless the changes are acceptable to the Superintendent of Insurance at the time of filing the prospectus under the Real Estate Act.

The bylaws can be amended only if such an amendment receives a majority of not less than three-quarters of the votes of all persons entitled to vote. Each strata lot has one vote. No addition to, amendment to, or repeal of a bylaw set out in the first or second schedules has any effect until the strata corporation gives notice to the Land Title Office in which the strata corporation is located. This office, in turn, will make reference to the notice on the deposited strata plans. Therefore, any prospective purchasers are able to ascertain the appropriate bylaws they would be subject to by searching the title at the proper Land Title Office.

Although the Condominium Act provides that strata corporations formed under the previous act will be governed by the new act, there are two exceptions. First, their bylaws will remain the same, unless they are amended, and they may be amended only with a three-quarters majority.

Second, the unit entitlement (i.e., each owner's share in the common property) of each strata lot will remain the same, but it will govern only the share in the common property and the contribution to common expenses. Under the old act, unit entitlement also affected the voting rights, but this is no longer so, as each strata lot now has only one vote.

2.   The strata corporation

As soon as a strata plan is filed in the Land Title Office, a corporation is created and the members of this corporation are the owners of the various units. The strata corporation is a legal entity and may sue and be sued. It also should, through the officers of the corporation, obtain and maintain insurance on the buildings and the common facilities, review annually the adequacy of the insurance, and pay the premiums on the policies.

In addition, the strata corporation shall establish a fund for administrative purposes as well as a contingency reserve fund, and raise the amount so determined by levying contributions on the owners in proportion to their unit entitlements. Other duties and powers of the strata corporation are set out as paragraphs 2 and 3 in the first schedule of the bylaws.

As previously mentioned, the owner of each strata lot is entitled to one vote at meetings of the strata corporation. However, the Condominium Act provides that where a strata owner's interest is subject to a registered mortgage, the mortgage may provide that a lender may vote in any matter relating to insurance, maintenance, finance, or other matters affecting the security for the mortgage.

To do so, the lender has to give written notice of the mortgage to the strata corporation and written notice of the intention to exercise the power to vote to the owner at least one day prior to the meeting. This right to vote is usually taken by the lender in most condominium mortgages today.

In the event of the breakup or destruction of the buildings of the strata corporation, the assets are apportioned in accordance with a schedule attached to the strata plan. This schedule is not necessarily the same as the unit entitlement.

The strata corporation is similar in operation to any other type of corporation and, of course, has a board of directors known as the council of the strata corporation. The duties of the council and the regulations governing its conduct are set out in paragraphs 4 to 21 of the first schedule of the bylaws. Any member of the strata corporation (i.e., any owner) is eligible for election to the council.

3. Information that should be obtained prior to purchase

Legislation requires the vendors of five or more strata lots to prepare a prospectus in the same way that a vendor of five or more lots in a subdivision is obliged to do. This prospectus provides a lot of necessary information and is, therefore, a very important document to the purchaser.

In addition to giving the particulars of the vendor, including previous history and some financial details, it discloses financing details for the strata project, information about the common facilities and services that will be provided to the project, and information with regard to transportation, unit entitlement, monthly contributions, parking arrangements, management contracts, schools, and police.

The information contained in the prospectus will form the basis of a contract which will be enforceable as long as the purchaser has been provided with a copy and has been given the opportunity to read it. A receipt to this effect will be requested by the vendor prior to a sale being written up. As can be seen, a prospectus is potentially a very important document and should be read and understood before any purchase is entered into.

Since a prospectus is required only from a person selling five or more lots within a subdivision, it will not be provided by the live-in owner who has decided to sell the unit and move out.

As a prospective purchaser, you should also be concerned with the boundaries of the unit that you are buying. These boundaries are set out in the strata plan when it is filed in the Land Title Office. If a plan is not available for inspection at the time of the signing of the interim agreement, you should insert a "subject to" clause or a representation as to what is included in the unit. This is important as it allows you to know what portions of the condominium project are yours alone and what portions of the condominium project you share with the other owners.

For example, in a row housing type of condominium project, each unit may have attached to it a patio, a backyard, and a garage. If you, as condominium unit owner, are the exclusive owner of your patio, backyard, and garage, you have a legal right to require that other people not use or interfere with your ownership of these amenities. On the other hand, if these items are common elements, your right to the enjoyment of these items is no greater than the right of any other unit owner in the condominium project.

Unless otherwise stipulated in the strata plan, the common boundary of a strata lot either with any other strata lot or with common property is the centre of the floor, wall, or ceiling — as the case may be. This centreline division, which is the most common, allows you, the strata lot owner, to deal with the inside walls as your own property for the purposes of decorating, hanging pictures, etc., while the outside walls are the property and responsibility of the strata corporation. In this manner the strata corporation is able to control the outside appearance of the whole project.

Water pipes, heating ducts, electrical wiring, and other apparatus passing between the strata lots are normally considered common property, and the standard first schedule of the bylaws, paragraph 1, sub-paragraph (a), permits the strata corporation and its agents to enter any strata lot for the purpose of inspecting and repairing such items.

Another matter you should investigate before purchasing is the amount of your monthly contribution toward common expenses. The common expenses are expenses incurred by the strata corporation in running the condominium project and maintaining the common areas. Such expenses include fire insurance for the units; liability insurance; heating, lighting, and maintenance of the common areas; salaries for the caretaker and other help; and other obligations that the strata corporation may have.

In addition, the Condominium Act provides that the strata corporation shall establish a contingency reserve fund for the purpose of providing for unforeseen future expenses.

The council of the strata corporation will establish a cash requirement every year to meet such expenses and each owner is assessed on proportionate share of this cash requirement, based on the unit entitlement. Strata lot owners' contributions to this cash requirement are usually made by way of monthly payments. It is important for you, as a prospective owner, to determine the amount of this monthly contribution for budgeting purposes.

If the strata lot owner defaults in making the monthly contributions toward the common expenses, the strata corporation has various remedies. It may either sue the owner, cut off the owner's utility services (this requires a majority resolution of the members of the corporation), or register a certificate in the Land Title Office showing the amount owing and the legal description of the lot of that owner. After one month's notice to the owner, the strata corporation may then make an application to the court for an order for the sale of the strata lot.

If the owner disputes the liability, the Condominium Act has provisions for submitting the dispute to arbitration, and this decision is binding if ratified by the court. In addition, no conveyance of an owner's interest, whether by assignment, lease, agreement for sale, or otherwise, can be registered in the Land Title Office unless the document is accompanied by a "certificate of full payment."

This certificate is issued by the strata corporation, stating that no money is owing to it, whether for contribution to common expenses, for fines for breach of the bylaws, for unsatisfied judgments against the owner, for pecuniary awards of an arbitrator, or for anything else. As purchaser of a strata lot, you should not only obtain a "certificate of full payment" for land registry purposes, but you would also, for your own information, obtain a certificate containing the following information:

(a) The amount of any contribution determined as the contribution of the owner

(b) The manner in which the contribution was payable

(c) The extent to which the contribution has been paid by the owner

(d) The amount of any money expended on behalf of the owner and not recovered

A purchaser also needs to know what amounts in (a) and (c) constitute the contribution toward administrative expenses and what amount is the contribution toward the establishment of the contingency reserve fund.

The bylaws, of course, should also be reviewed to ensure that you can live in accordance with them. They may, for example, contain restrictions on the number of persons who are allowed to live in each unit, or prohibit or restrict the keeping of pets. Any of these could be very important to you as a prospective purchaser.

Since the strata corporation, in most instances, is run by the owners who perform their duties for the corporation in their spare time, it is common for it to enter into a management agreement with a full-time management company specializing in providing full-time services to strata corporations. This is often also a requirement of the lending institution providing the mortgage money as an attempt to provide the strata owners with management that has intimate knowledge of the workings of the condominiums and to establish a workable, reasonable, and efficient strata lot government.

Such management contracts can, under the Condominium Act, be cancelled by either party on three months' notice, provided that cancellation by the strata corporation requires a special resolution (three-quarters majority by owners). By obtaining a copy of the management agreement, a strata lot owner or a prospective purchaser can become familiar with all the rights and duties of the manager.

The Condominium Act requires the strata corporation to obtain and maintain insurance on the buildings, the common facilities, and any insurable improvements owned by the strata corporation for the full replacement value. The managers of the strata corporation are required to review the adequacy of such insurance annually and to pay the premiums on the policies. A prospective purchaser should, prior to the completion of the purchase, obtain confirmation of such insurance, as well as a copy of the policies.

Insurance in a condominium project is a complex matter because of the common property and the interdependence of the owners of the strata lots. The basic policy owned by the strata corporation will cover the replacement of the strata lots and the common property.

It should also contain public liability insurance against personal injury or damage to the property of other people. For example, a guest of one of the strata lot owners who slips and falls on a path of ice that should have been cleared may have a claim against the strata corporation or the strata lot owner or both. The strata corporation may carry this type of insurance for itself, but the policy may not necessarily provide any insurance for the owner. In such an event, the owner should also carry liability insurance.

In addition, the owner should make sure that the contents of the unit are insured, as this is probably not covered in the strata corporation policy either. Contents insurance provides a strata lot owner with protection against damage to the contents such as furniture, appliances, art objects, carpets, cameras, and furs.

In addition, a strata lot owner may have made various improvements to the strata lot which may not have been covered by the fire insurance policy obtained by the condominium corporation. Such improvements would include wall panelling, finishing the basement, or installing built-in shelving units or extra cabinets. If such improvements have been made, a separate and additional fire insurance policy may be required.

As previously mentioned, the Condominium Act has been in force in British Columbia for a short period of time. The experience, although limited, has been that these types of dwelling units have increased in value in the same proportion, on the average, as fully-detached houses. It stands to reason that this trend will continue under present conditions, since the three main ingredients affecting prices — namely, increasing demand for accommodation, escalating land costs, and escalating costs of labor and materials — are all present in the condominium just as they are in the detached house, although perhaps in slightly different proportions.

c. COOPERATIVES

A cooperative refers to an incorporated company which is the owner of property where the shareholders are entitled to occupy all or a portion of the property. An example is an apartment building where the shareholders are entitled to live in their own specified apartments.

A "purchaser" of such an "apartment" enters into a lease with the company for the specific dwelling unit. At the same time, the purchaser buys shares in the company. The company then manages the apartment and makes sure that the gardening is done, the hallways are vacuumed and lighted, the elevators are running, etc.

For this service, the leaseholder pays a monthly maintenance fee. This monthly maintenance fee should be enough both to cover the maintenance and upkeep of the building and to include a small reserve for contingencies. It is not intended that the company make a profit, or the shareholders expect dividends on their shares, as with a normal corporation. The ownership of the shares merely serves to give the owners a say in the running of the company and hence, through it, the running of the apartment.

As with normal corporations, the shareholders elect a board of directors whose job it is to run the corporation and thus make sure that the apartment is properly managed.

As with strata lots, legislation requires a real estate prospectus to be filed where two or more units of the cooperative are to be sold or leased. As mentioned before, this document is a very important document for the purchaser. So, what I have already said about condominiums requiring the prospectus applies here, too.

Before purchasing an interest in a cooperative, you should thoroughly read and understand not only the prospectus, but also, if available, the memorandum and articles of the company.

161

The articles of the company are the bylaws of the company and set down the procedures for calling meetings of shareholders, the quorum needed, voting procedures, how distribution is to be made in winding up of the company, and requirements for share transfers (i.e., any restrictions on whom they can be sold to).

In addition, you should find out what the monthly maintenance fee is and request financial statements so that the financial condition of the company can be determined. The financial condition of the company has, through the monthly maintenance charge, a direct effect on a leaseholder, as any deficiencies can be made up only through an increased monthly charge.

The leases granted are usually long-term leases, commonly 50 years and more. Financing for the cooperative purchase is difficult and is one of the drawbacks to the scheme.

A purchaser could conceivably obtain financing by giving as collateral a mortgage of the lease and lodging the shares in trust. Although there is nothing wrong with such an arrangement when properly done, very few lenders feel secure enough to accept it and, consequently, such mortgage money is very scarce.

The other way to finance the cooperative purchase is for the company to take out one mortgage on the whole property and then to have each "owner" assume a pro rata portion of such mortgage. This is a cumbersome and inflexible method, as it is very difficult to fit such an arrangement to the needs of the individual purchaser. Some people may want an 85% mortgage while other people may want no mortgage at all. Yet, if one "owner" should default in his or her obligation to make mortgage payments, the other members must make up the default or be faced with foreclosure.

Prior to the introduction of the Condominium Act, cooperative apartment ownership was used to achieve the same basic result that the Condominium Act has now accomplished. When renting became unprofitable and many older apartments were converted to strata lots and sold, giving tenants a choice of either purchasing or moving, the government passed legislation to effectively stop such conversions. This again brought the cooperatives into vogue.

Their new-found popularity was short-lived, however, as municipal approval is now required for residential leases of more than three years (another blow to the freedom of the property owner).

As it is questionable whether this would prohibit a series of options to lease from being given, each lease (containing a renewal option) being for no more than three years, it may very well be that cooperatives can weather the storm and become a popular vehicle again.

All in all the cooperative purchase is a very specialized type of ownership, containing many pitfalls for the unwary.

In addition to the items discussed here, there are many other items that should be investigated. Do the number of shares which you, as a purchaser, get give you proper pro rata representation? Are the real property taxes which are assessed against the corporation pro rated among the various owners and, if so, on what basis, or does the four-bedroom penthouse with a view pay the same amount of taxes as the studio suite on the bottom floor facing the lane?

In short, if a purchase of this sort is contemplated, you should really seek professional help.

d. LEASE LOT OWNERSHIP

Governments at all levels have marketed lease lots in the past. The theory was that, instead of selling freehold lots (lots to which title could be obtained), they would sell leasehold lots (lots to which the title would stay in the name

163

of the government or municipality, which would grant a long-term lease (usually 99 years) to the purchaser) for less money, thus helping to keep the cost of accommodation down. At the same time this was done, the difference on, for example, a $59 000 lot would be approximately $4 000 to $4 500. Therefore, instead of selling a freehold lot for $59 000, they would sell a lease lot for, maybe, $54 500.

In most instances, the lots were sold directly to builders who, in turn, built houses on them and placed them on the market in the $180 000 to $200 000 range. The cost of construction for an identical home built on a lease lot or on a freehold lot would, of course, be the same. In circumstances such as this the principle behind the leasehold lot — saving the purchaser money — becomes rather ridiculous. This message appears to have been heeded and many municipalities have allowed their leaseholders the opportunity to buy out their leases and convert their properties to freehold.

The leasehold lot is basically that — a leased lot. The lease is usually a long-term lease and allows you to build and generally treat the property as your own. Although not all conventional lenders are prepared to accept mortgages of leases as security for the advance of mortgage money, a sufficient number have done this so that the supply of mortgage money for such lots is adequate. This could be partly because some lenders will charge a slightly higher interest rate to compensate them for accepting this type of investment for their mortgage money.

When the lease expires, the land and all of the improvements made to it revert to the grantor of the lease — in most instances, without compensation. Except for these basic differences and exceptions in the individual leases, a lease can, for all intents and purposes, be treated as a freehold lot.

e. TRAILERS AND MOBILE HOMES

These do not really fall within the scope of this book. They are, however, alternative forms of accommodation which can be obtained at more reasonable prices.

The trailer or mobile home is treated as personal property and is separate from the land. Financing is usually arranged through finance companies rather than through the conventional mortgage lenders. The financing is secured either by conditional sales contracts or by chattel mortgages registered in Victoria.

Before purchasing a trailer or mobile home, you should make arrangements for its location. Even if you own your own land, municipal bylaws may prevent you from moving the trailer onto your land and using it as a home. Other considerations for the location of a mobile home are power hookup and disposal of sewage. So, you would be wise to investigate these matters prior to purchase.

8

WHAT YOU NEED TO KNOW ABOUT SELLING YOUR HOME

a. INTRODUCTION

Much of this book may seem to be directed at the purchaser of property. This is not really so. Remember, before there can be a purchaser there must also be a vendor, and nearly everything that the purchaser does affects the vendor: if the purchaser pays, the vendor receives payment; if the purchaser receives vendor financing, the vendor provides the financing; when the purchaser obtains possession, the vendor provides possession; if fire insurance is owned by the purchaser, the vendor's fire insurance should be cancelled, and so on.

As the majority of these problems are discussed elsewhere in this book, this chapter is not meant to provide an exhaustive checklist for the vendor. But it deals with some problems that are of primary concern to the vendor.

After you have made the basic decision to sell your home, three other matters must be determined before you put it on the market:

(a) The asking price

(b) How the purchase price is to be received

(c) How to go about finding the purchaser

b. HOW MUCH SHOULD YOU ASK FOR YOUR HOME?

All vendors of homes naturally wish to obtain the best possible price. On the other hand, they must be realistic and not put such a high price on their homes that prospective purchasers will be

166

discouraged from inspecting or making offers on the property.

On the other hand, the owners should not determine the price by what they feel they need to sell their houses for. That is no guide at all and would probably be either too high or too low. There is only one sure guide to follow — the *fair market value* of the house.

Most home owners think they have a fairly good idea of what their property is worth, primarily from information on what they think other, similar houses in the area have sold for. However, you should keep in mind that the asking price is not the selling price of the house. The vendor advertises the asking price, but not the selling price. Even if the vendor did disclose the selling price, it would probably be higher than what was actually received since no one likes to admit to coming down too far, if at all.

It is, therefore, always advisable to get second opinions from someone who is qualified and knowledgeable in the real estate market. One such obvious person, of course, is the real estate agent, who can be of great assistance in this area. It should be pointed out, however, that some agents will suggest whatever market price they feel will induce the owner to list with them, although they have no real hope of selling at that price. In fact, a far too common guise of agents who are attempting to induce you to sign a multiple listing agreement (higher commission) is to "promise" you a higher price.

To test agents' sincerity, request that they set an upset price below which their commissions would decrease proportionally to the sales price. If they accept, incorporate the terms in the listing agreement.

Also, do not sign listing agreements with long expiry dates. If the agent works out satisfactorily, the listing can always be renewed.

Remember, however, that before setting a sales price, it is wise to get several opinions, if possible, or even to visit open houses in the area in order to get a proper feel for the prevailing market prices.

Even if the market prices can be established with reasonable certainty, it would be wise to obtain an appraisal of your property from a qualified and reputable appraisal firm, the name of which can be easily obtained from your bank. The cost of such an appraisal for the average home is approximately $150. Not only would this give you peace of mind, but it is also cheap insurance if there is any doubt as to what a proper market price would be, so that your property will not be undersold.

The appraisal will also provide information about the replacement value of your property and will give you a positive point of reference. You will know your price is competitive regardless of what the purchaser may say, and you will be able to meet the shrewdest purchaser on better than equal terms. It would be one of the wisest investments you, as a vendor, could make.

c. HOW SHOULD YOU BE PAID?

This is not a trite question, as there are two basic alternatives involved:

1. Cashed out

You can ask to be "cashed out" (i.e., either the purchaser pays all cash for clear title or pays cash for your equity and is allowed to assume your mortgage or mortgages).

Although a transaction is described as "all cash for clear title," it does not necessarily mean that all the purchaser's money is sitting in a bank account waiting to be spent on a house. As a matter of fact, relatively few transactions are of this kind. It merely means that the purchaser wants clear title and will look after his or her own financing.

Before accepting an offer on those terms, you, as vendor, should make sure that you can, in fact, deliver clear title. If you have a mortgage on your property, you should make certain that such a mortgage can be paid out. Unless there is a specific provision in the mortgage, you may find that the lender is not prepared to let you pay the mortgage out at all, or only if, for example, you are prepared to pay a penalty equivalent to six months' interest on the mortgage. If that is the case, you may be better off finding a way to structure the sale as a cash-to-mortgage transaction.

You should also be aware of the "sales" clause before considering a cash-to-mortgage offer. Some mortgages contain a "sales" clause whereby the lender reserves the right to call the mortgage if the property is sold.

If this is the case with your mortgage, you can accept a cash-to-mortgage deal only if the purchaser is approved by the lender. Otherwise they have the right to "call in" the mortgage. This will usually happen if the current mortgage rates are higher than the mortgage rate contained in the old mortgage.

However, should the mortgage rate contained in the old mortgage be higher than the current mortgage rates the lender will, in all likelihood, approve the new purchaser if otherwise satisfied with the mortgage security. If the lender chooses to call in the mortgage, a prepayment penalty cannot be charged.

You should also be conscious of the fact that the mortgage that is being assumed was initially a contract between you and the mortgage company and, if the purchaser defaults on the mortgage, you would still be liable to pay the debt. This can be avoided if the original lender is prepared to release you from your obligation to pay. You will, however, usually find that the lender is not prepared to give such a release and you must find other ways to protect yourself.

The effect of this is to give you a claim against the purchaser for any expenses or liability that you may incur if the purchaser is sued by the lender. Second, you should do a credit check on the purchaser. Your bank can help you in this regard, and the charge is only around $2 to $5. If the purchaser's credit looks shaky, a guarantor should be sought. Third, you should make sure that there is some margin of equity in the home over and above the mortgage that is being assumed, thus minimizing any liability to yourself.

2. You supply financing

You may supply some, if not all, of the financing for the purchaser. This type of financing has already been dealt with in chapter 6, under the heading Vendor Financing, and you should refer to it for further details.

There is one interesting tax angle you should know about in relation to vendor financing. Any interest earned from such a mortgage is income and, depending on your tax position, it may very well be to your advantage to ask more for your home (as the capital gain on the sale of your home is tax free) but offer a lower interest rate on the financing.

Similarly, in situations where there is joint ownership and the individuals involved are in different income tax brackets, the sale should be structured in such a way that the person with the higher income tax bracket receives the down payment while the person with the lower income tax bracket provides the financing so that the interest income is taxed at the lower rate.

d. HOW TO FIND A PURCHASER

There are two basic ways of approaching the real estate market in the hope of finding a purchaser.

1. Sell it yourself

You can attempt to sell the house yourself. To attract purchasers, you can place a sign on your front lawn and/or an advertisement in the local newspaper. If a purchaser is found in this manner the only costs will have been your time and effort and the cost of the sign and/or the advertisement.

Finally, you should have sufficient background in real estate to be able to write a proper and legally binding interim agreement. If you are the least bit unsure of your ground in this area, you should consult a lawyer, notary, or someone else experienced in real estate matters who would also be able to hold the deposit in trust. If you are able to find a purchaser in this manner you will, of course, save the cost of the real estate commission, which, on a $200 000 house, at 5% or 7% is $10 000 or $14 000.

Remember that most purchasers are aware of this as well and will expect to share somewhat in the savings. Consequently, the savings may not be as great as they would appear at first glance.

When placing an advertisement in the paper, you must follow certain rules. In order to be effective, there must be a proper sequence of thought and of interest in the way the advertisement is structured.

The information should always be supplied in the order of its importance to the person who will read it. Since the majority of purchasers are looking for homes in one particular district within certain price ranges, these two items should be the focal point, that is, in the first line and preferably in the larger print.

On the other hand, if the advertisement is for a lower-priced home, maybe the cash required and the monthly payment would appeal more to the prospective purchaser and, therefore, should be headlined instead.

If the headline passes the test by catching the attention of a prospective purchaser, the number of bedrooms should be given next, for that is probably the next concern; then the style of the house and the size (square footage of livable area only);

171

the buyer's attention — for example, views, swimming pools, the amount of down payment needed (*only* if very small), etc. Also mention the fact that the property is for sale by the owner. The ad below is one example.

Use adjectives with discretion. Too many will spoil the effect. Don't oversell. The truth will become apparent when the house is seen. When showing your home, take the role of a courteous host rather than an aggressive salesperson. Do not lead the prospects. Follow them so their view of the rooms is not blocked.

MEADOWBROOK $182 000

4 bdrm. rancher, 1 800 sq. ft., separate dining and living room, wall-to-wall throughout, efficient kitchen with family room adjoining, built-in stove and oven, 2 baths, master bdrm. en suite, carport, workshop, lots of storage, large fully landscaped lot. Private sale, no agents. Please phone ——

First impressions are very important, so don't spoil them by standing in their way. Similarly, make sure all areas are lighted so that prospects do not have to fumble their way around. Open closet doors for them so they can see the size; they may be a little diffident about opening them themselves.

It is also an excellent idea to prepare an information sheet which can be casually handed to the prospect when the introductions have been made. This sheet should contain, for example, the address, price, age of the home, lot size, taxes, existing financing if assumable, dimensions of the various rooms, total square footage, type of heating and heating costs, number of bathrooms, nearest school locations, bus services, nearest grocery store, etc. (See the book *For Sale by Owner*, also published by Self-Counsel Press.)

Finally, you should make a critical assessment of the house the way a prospect would by walking through the house and garden and, with a critical eye, making a list of things that need attention. Every house has such "things," but many of these can be attended to very quickly and cheaply.

Make sure the dishes are done and the beds are made before showing the house. This, of course, would apply equally whether the house is being sold by the owner or through an agent.

2. Use of a real estate agent

The second approach is to market the house through a real estate agent. Today, the majority of residential real estate transactions occur through the use of real estate agents who can perform a number of basic services for you, including advising you on the pricing of the property.

The real estate agent may also already have access to prospective customers and, if not, should spend time obtaining them. If you don't feel your agent is doing a good job, you can ask to be released from the listing agreement. Most home owners do not realize that some companies will voluntarily release a vendor from obligations under a listing agreement if that vendor is genuinely unhappy with the agent. A good agent will assist and advise throughout the transaction, from the interim agreement to completion, and even after.

Real estate agents are paid fees or commissions for their services. The fees can vary from 3½% to 10% of the gross sale price, depending on the agent and what is being sold. Although some real estate agents charge only 3½% commission on the sale of a home, the "standard" commission for an exclusive listing is 5%, while a multiple listing is 7%, and the "standard" commission for bare land is 10%. These percentages are calculated on the gross sale price. Once the value of the property exceeds $100 000, the standard commission is reduced to 2½% on the excess.

Since the commission is paid on a percentage of the sale price, it is in the mutual interest of both the agent and the vendor to obtain the highest possible price for the home. However, the agent, who does not earn any income until the sale is transacted, may encourage you to accept a lower price for a home in order to complete a sale.

In this respect, there is a conflict of interest between you and the agent, and it is at this stage that you should have an independent appraisal to refer to. What you should do if the agent has listed your home at a much higher price than was realistic has already been covered (see section **b.**).

Why was the word "standard" placed in quotes when referring to commission rates? "Standard" in this case does not mean legal. There is no obligation on your part to accept the "standard" commission rate of 5%, 7%, or 10%. This rate is "suggested" by your friendly real estate board of which your real estate company is probably a member. Sometimes it is, however, possible to bargain with these rates. Don't forget, however, that in the end, it is the commission that is the incentive.

Some real estate companies do not adhere to the "standard" rate at all and one company in Vancouver charges only 3¼%. Remember, the commission may represent a substantial portion of the equity in your home. Try to calculate it yourself. But remember also that it is the net price to *you* (no matter what the commission) that should be the determining factor.

As the real estate agent is the agent of the vendor, the law of agency requires that the agent be authorized by the vendor to make certain representations. The information contained in these representations is supplied by the vendor who, accordingly, must be careful to be accurate in describing the property to the agent. The agent and vendor could, otherwise, become involved in a lawsuit for misrepresentation. For a further discussion on the role of the real estate agent, please refer to chapter 3.

e. THE LISTING AGREEMENT

An agent, before agreeing to work on a property, will require that you enter into a binding arrangement for a commission in the event of a sale. This agreement is referred to as the listing agreement. There are three types of listing agreements available. These are:

(a) The open listing

(b) The exclusive listing

(c) The multiple listing

1. The open listing

Under an open listing the vendor agrees to pay the real estate agent a specified rate of commission if the real estate agent finds a purchaser for the property.

The agent in an open listing does not have an exclusive authority over the property and, accordingly, you may enter into several open listing agreements with several agents.

Naturally an agent would prefer more control over the property before agreeing to spend much time on it or to spend money in advertising it with the possibility that someone else could receive the commission. So, in most instances, only an agent who has a good prospect in mind will accept an open listing.

The situation may be alleviated a bit if you agree to reimburse the agent with an open listing agreement for the bona fide advertising expenses incurred while the agent is attempting to sell the property (in case that agent is not the one who sells the house).

2. The exclusive listing

The exclusive listing is similar in form to the open listing with the exception that the exclusive listing gives the real estate agent the exclusive right to sell the property for a specified period of time. The vendor, again, is then stuck with the agent for that period of time. However, as mentioned, the practice (at least, with some real estate companies) is to allow the vendor to cancel if not happy with the agent. To protect yourself in this

175

situation, you should request a letter confirming the cancellation. The sales representative's word is not enough.

If the property is sold by anyone else other than the agent during this period of time or if the property is sold to someone who was introduced to the property by the real estate agent before the expiration of the listing agreement, the agent is entitled to a commission.

This is the most usual type of listing agreement, and the real estate agent will usually work harder under this type of arrangement than under the open listing, as a commission is assured in a sale.

3. The multiple listing

The third type of listing agreement in common use today is the multiple listing. This type of listing is provided by an association of agents who have agreed to pool their resources not only to increase the supply of homes that they have to show to prospective purchasers, but also to increase the number of prospective purchasers that they may have available to introduce to willing vendors.

You should, however, be aware that because the commission split is bigger, the agent has a vested interest in putting your home on multiple listing. When a listing is given, all the particulars, usually including a picture, are fed to the central association which then distributes them to its members. The alleged advantage of this type of listing is that it gives a property more coverage.

As already mentioned, the fee for such broader coverage is usually 2% of the gross sale price above the standard exclusive commission. Unless you are in a real hurry, don't start off with multiple listing. Start off with exclusive listing. Your agent will be happy to change to multiple any time even though your exclusive contract has not expired, and your house might sell at the lower rate of commission. Also, an exclusive listing can be written for a shorter period and the agent can be changed if not satisfactory. The minimum multiple listing is for three months.

In many instances, depending on the present market and the real estate agent involved, it may not be necessary to go to a multiple listing in order to obtain a broader coverage than a straight exclusive listing gives.

First, many listing agents will hold an open house for their own agents shortly after a new exclusive listing is obtained. In this manner all salespersons in the real estate agent's office are exposed to the property.

Second, most agents, regardless of the company involved, will cooperate with one another on exclusive listings and split the commission in the event of a sale. Accordingly, many agents will hold "agents' open houses" where other salespeople and agents working in approximately the same area are invited to attend so that they can become acquainted with what is available on the market.

Third, there are other ways of getting wider advertising than multiple listing. For example, Block Bros. Realtors, one of the largest real estate companies in British Columbia, offer a service they call N.R.S. (National Real Estate Service). This service consists of a printed catalogue of listings divided into areas with all the particulars of the properties in these areas, including square footage, number of rooms, price, financing, and a picture. These catalogues are printed weekly and distributed not only in Block Bros.' own offices but also to associated brokers for coast-to-coast exposure.

The additional fee for a listing in this catalogue (over and above the normal exclusive listing fee) is 0.5% of the first $100 000. The fee for both the N.R.S. and multiple listing is 7.3% of the first $100 000 and 2.5% thereafter for the Lower Mainland. The rate may vary for other areas of the country and should be checked first with Block Bros.

Before leaving the section on listing agreements you should note that many listing agreements *and* forms of interim agreements provide that a commission is payable for arranging a contract. That is, even if the sale, for some reason, is not concluded, the commission would still be payable. To protect yourself, when signing such a listing or interim agreement, you should insist that the commission become payable only if and when the transaction is completed and make sure you make the necessary amendments to the listing or interim agreement to accomplish this.

Another potential problem regarding the commission is that the vendor's copy of the interim agreement states that the agent may keep whatever deposit is paid for the agent's troubles. Provided it is not the vendor's fault that the transaction is not completed, it is only fair that the vendor receive at least part of the deposit, since, in all likelihood, the vendor will suffer as much loss as the real estate agent if the purchase is not completed.

Again, it is suggested that an amendment be made to the agreement along these lines: "In the event the sale is not completed through no fault of the vendor, the vendor and the agent herein agree to equally share the deposit money claimed as liquidated damages," or such similar wording. Check the interim agreement and make the appropriate amendment.

f. THE DEPOSIT

Contrary to popular belief, the deposit is not necessarily required to have a binding interim agreement. As a matter of fact, the main function of the deposit is to commit the purchaser in an attempt to guarantee performance and to show good faith in the transaction. Therefore, the amount of the deposit is completely flexible.

As the vendor, naturally you will want as large a deposit as possible, since, if a purchaser fails to complete, the deposit, or part of it, may be forfeited to you. Therefore, the larger the amount of the deposit, the greater incentive for the purchaser to complete. Real estate agents also prefer large deposits. If an agent is involved, normally that agent will keep the deposit. This does not mean the money belongs to the agent, but only that the agent holds it "in trust" pending completion of the deal. After completion, the real estate agent applies the deposit toward the commission payable. Therefore, it is not uncommon for the agent to attempt to obtain a deposit at least equal to the amount of the real commission.

The provisions of the Real Estate Act govern the real estate agent's trust account. The deposit kept in the trust account cannot be disbursed until one of the following events has occurred:

(a) The transaction is completed.

(b) Both the vendor and the purchaser provide the real estate agent with the same instructions as to the disbursement of the funds.

If there is a dispute as to who is entitled to the deposit, the Real Estate Act provides that the agent may pay the money into court for a determination as to who is entitled to receive it. And this is exactly what happens in practice. When the deposit is paid directly to the vendor, there is no law that says the vendor must hold the deposit in trust. The vendor is free to use the money as he or she pleases unless the interim agreement provides otherwise.

g. ACCEPTING THE OFFER

This is an area which basically involves contract law. Please refer to chapter 2 for guidance here.

Most standard forms of interim agreements contain a clause at the bottom for the signature of the vendor. This clause serves two purposes. First, the vendor accepts the offer to purchase and, by doing so, becomes bound by the terms of the offer. Second, there is an agreement between the vendor and the real estate agent for the payment of the real estate commission and an outline of the mechanics of this payment.

As mentioned previously, you should add to or alter this clause so that the commission will become payable only if the transaction is completed. Likewise, if the transaction is not completed due to the fault of the purchaser, provisions should be made so that the deposit is shared between you and the agent. Of course, if no real estate agent is involved in the transaction, the second item should be deleted from the offer and initialled by the parties.

In considering the offer to purchase, you should satisfy yourself that:

(a) The warranties and representations (if any) made by yourself in the interim agreement are true and correct.

(b) You can comply with the various obligations imposed on you (e.g., clear title, completion, and possession dates) within the required time. When you are purchasing another home, you should make sure that the completion date for the sale of your house is far enough in advance for you to obtain the proceeds and use these proceeds in completing the purchase of your new home. At the same time, you should also make certain that you are not required to give up possession of your old home before you are in a position to move.

It should also be mentioned here that if the property is to be vacant for a period of longer than 10 to 15 days, the "standard" fire insurance policy contains a provision requiring the owner of the property to advise the insurance company. Therefore, if you are selling your property and moving out 10 to 15 days before the completion date, the insurance company should be notified so that it can issue an endorsement to the insurance policy, commonly called a vacancy permit. There is usually no charge for the issuance of such a permit, but, if it is not done, the insurance company could refuse to pay should a claim arise.

One final note: Remember, if you want to change any clause in the interim agreement, you may do so by making the necessary change, initialling the change and, of course, signing the interim agreement. This will constitute a counter-offer by you, which the purchaser may either accept or reject. If the purchaser rejects the counter-offer, you cannot later accept the original offer unless it is re-submitted to you by the purchaser.

Once the offer is accepted by you, a binding agreement of sale is made. Further documentation is required to complete the sale — and that is the subject of the next chapter.

9

LAWYERS AND NOTARIES —
WHAT THEY CAN AND CANNOT
DO FOR YOU

a. WHY IT IS WISE TO CONSULT A LAWYER

Real estate today is expensive. As mentioned before, because of the money involved, the purchase of a home is probably the largest investment you will make in your life. If it's a good transaction and everything goes well, it will probably be the best and most rewarding investment of your life. However, unless you are careful, it can very easily turn out to be a disastrous experience.

An average home today in the Greater Vancouver area is priced at around $230 000. With that kind of money at stake, it makes sense to obtain competent help and guidance in the real estate transaction to make sure you obtain good title to the property being purchased. What follows is an example of someone who was "penny wise" but "pound foolish."

Penny McScrooge had, through sheer hard work and frugality, managed to save $32 000 for the down payment of her dream — her own house. Through an advertisement in the paper she contacted Fast Eddie O'Greedy who was selling his house himself.

After Fast Eddie had shown her his house, Penny decided that this was the house for her. She was particularly impressed with the new recreation room in the basement which Fast Eddie had just completed. As Fast Eddie's equity in the house was $32 000, Penny signed an interim agreement agreeing to pay cash to Fast Eddie's nice 8% first mortgage.

Since Fast Eddie "knew" something about conveyancing, he gallantly offered to help Penny have the title transferred into her name so that she could save some of those "dreadful" legal expenses. He produced for her a statement from the mortgage company showing the balance outstanding and they managed to settle the "adjustment" matters between them.

From his old legal documents, Fast Eddie then prepared a title transfer document which he had signed in front of a notary public. He then completed the balance of the necessary documentation, all of which he gave to Ms. McScrooge.

The next morning, after having paid Fast Eddie his $32 000, Penny happily trotted down the Land Title Office and submitted her documents for registration. Thirty days later, after having moved into the house, she received a demand letter from a lawyer acting on behalf of a client who had a registered judgment against Fast Eddie's property in the amount of $30 000. The gist of the letter was that she would have to pay the $30 000 or face foreclosure of her interest in the home.

In the same mail, she also received a demand letter from one of the major oil companies demanding that she immediately pay all *arrears* amounting to $370 for her hot water heater or face the possibility of having it removed. She immediately phoned the oil company, but, although they were sympathetic, they felt that since they had registered their conditional sales agreement against the title, she should have checked with them about the outstanding balance owing on the agreement before proceeding with the purchase.

Being somewhat concerned about the situation at this stage, Penny immediately rushed down to the Land Title Office in the hope of having these matters resolved. After double-checking the title, she noticed not only the notation about the conditional sales agreement in its awkward position on the title, but also the judgment and a builder's lien which had now been registered against the property for the amount of $18 000. Finally, Penny decided it was time to see a lawyer. Ms. Good, of the law firm Good, Better & Best, patiently explained the following to her.

Since the judgment was registered prior to the registration of her title transfer deed, her interest in the property was subject to the judgment, and she would have to pay it off in order to get good title to the property. She would have to use her own money or try to recover enough money from Fast Eddie to pay it off. Since Fast Eddie had left town without a forwarding address the latter solution didn't look promising.

The conditional sales agreement was also registered at the time she submitted her transfer of title. In addition to the arrears, there still was $400 owing on the principal. She, therefore, purchased the property subject to the registered conditional sales agreement and, unless she paid not only the arrears but also future payments, the oil company would be entitled to repossess the hot water heater.

The builder's lien had been filed by the people who had renovated the basement in order to put the house into a more saleable condition. Since they had not been paid, they were entitled to file a lien against the property as long as they did so within 30 days after they had completed their work. To have this lien discharged, it would cost Penny $1 800, 10% of the amount of the lien. Since Fast Eddie had mentioned to her that the work was done, she should have withheld this amount of money from the purchase price to protect herself. However, as she had not, she was still liable to pay it.

The mortgage that she assumed contained a clause in it permitting the mortgage company to call its mortgage if the property was sold. As the interest rates on the first mortgages had risen substantially over the 8% rate of Fast Eddie's mortgage, the mortgage company did not allow the mortgage to be assumed and wanted to be paid out. Although they were prepared to consider Penny's application for a new mortgage there was no guarantee that she would qualify, and, even if she did, it would be at the current rate of interest of 12%, meaning that she would have to pay approximately $265 more per month in interest.

In addition to all these expenses, the legal fees to clear the matter up at this point would probably be four to five times the original conveyancing fees, with absolutely no guarantee that any of the money that she had already paid to Fast Eddie could be recovered.

This example ends with Penny passing out and sliding on to the floor while Ms. Good frantically attempts to get hold of a doctor and ambulance!

Needless to say, these things do not happen to everyone purchasing property, but they do show you some of the things that can go wrong. The land registry system and conveyancing law are full of traps for the unwary. It would be sheer foolishness for anyone not having the proper experience or guidance to attempt to handle a conveyance alone (i.e., preparing, signing, and registering the documentation evidencing the transfer of the legal and/or beneficial title to the property). It is, therefore, strongly recommended that competent legal advice be obtained before you sign the interim agreement.

One way to find a competent lawyer is to ask friends and acquaintances in the real estate business for a recommendation. Another way is to phone the Canadian Bar Association, which has a lawyer referral service and will recommend lawyers practising in a particular field. Of course, there are always the Yellow Pages or your real estate agent, who may recommend a lawyer.

In any event, before retaining a lawyer, you should first determine that the lawyer does real estate work and, second, the approximate amount of the fees. You may not be able to get an exact figure, but, depending on the price range of the house, a ball park figure should be available. Normal conveyancing charges will be discussed later.

When dealing with a lawyer, remember that a lawyer is a legal advisor, not a business consultant. Thus, a lawyer will provide for the protection of a client's rights, but should not be expected to provide advice as to whether or not it is a good deal. A lawyer can offer a personal opinion and can help structure the deal but should not go beyond that. It is for this reason that a lawyer's answer to a question may very well be, "That is a business question and one that you will have to answer for yourself."

b. LAWYER OR NOTARY PUBLIC?

Many people do not realize that there is a difference between a lawyer and a notary public. A lawyer in British Columbia is automatically a notary public while a notary public is not necessarily a lawyer.

Real estate lawyers have training in preparing conveyancing documentation and practising law, including conveyancing law. Notaries have training in preparing conveyancing documents but cannot practise law and are not, therefore, formally qualified to provide legal opinion.

A person who retains a lawyer will usually pay extra for competent legal advice and for an opinion on the quality of the title. In view of the fact that the transaction represents a major undertaking for the purchaser and because the quality of the title is the essence of the transaction, a purchaser (or vendor) should give careful consideration to priorities and who can best represent these.

c. LEGAL FEES

A lawyer's bill, or for that matter, a notary public's bill, is comprised of two items — fees and disbursements. The fees are for the services rendered to the client. The disbursements represent reimbursement of charges for those expenditures made on the client's behalf to complete the transaction.

Such expenses would include funds paid to the Land Title Office to have the title transfer document or mortgage registered, funds paid to have the searches done, money spent obtaining photocopies of all relevant documentation on file, etc.

The largest of such expenses is probably the property transfer tax. (See section **b. 8.** in chapter 1 for this important discussion.) With the advent of the property transfer tax, the fees otherwise paid to the Land Title Office as disbursements in order to get the documents registered have become relatively minor. Some of the common registration fees are as follows:

- To register a transfer — $50

- To register a mortgage — $50

- Agreement for sale — $50

- Discharge of mortgage — $15

- Certificate of state of title (a document which lists all the charges against the property) — $10 per title

In a real estate transaction, it is customary for the purchaser to pay all the legal fees in connection with the conveyance of the property. If, however, the vendor has agreed to provide a clear title, any charges incurred in connection with clearing the title are the vendor's responsibility.

Similarly, it is customary for the mortgagor (borrower) to agree to be responsible for all legal fees incurred by the mortgagee (lender) in connection with any mortgage loan.

In standard conveyance and mortgage matters, the lawyer's fee is either negotiated, based on Supreme Court tariff, or set according to the lawyer's own standard fees. If the transaction is not ordinary, the lawyer's fee will vary from the tariff or standard fee depending on the purchase price of the property, the amount of time spent on the transaction, the difficulty of the particular transaction, and various other factors. The tariff set up under the Supreme Court Rules is as follows:

(a) 1% of the first $2 500 of the purchase price or principal mortgage amount, whichever is applicable, with a minimum of $25

(b) Thereafter, up to ½ of 1% on the next $12 500

(c) Thereafter, up to ¼ of 1% on any amounts over $15 000

Under this tariff, a $50 000 house would incur legal fees of $175.

The standard fee for most lawyers practising in the Vancouver area who do not follow the Supreme Court tariff is based on the following:

> $12.50 basic charge plus ½ of 1% of the amount of the transaction up to $50 000 plus $17.50 or proportionate amount thereof per $10 000 thereafter

So, the fee for conveying a $50 000 piece of property would be $262.50 plus disbursements, and for a $100 000 purchase it would be $387.50 plus disbursements. In instances where the conveyancing lawyer is also acting for the mortgage company, the fee on the mortgage is customarily reduced approximately one-third, depending upon the amount of the mortgage.

Recent changes in the law society regulations now prohibit lawyers, due to the potential conflict of interest, from acting for both the mortgage company and the borrower unless both parties agree in writing. This same situation also applies to a lawyer acting for a vendor and a purchaser in the same transaction, unless the lawyer is simply clearing title.

Similarly, if the purchase price is secured by a mortgage back to the vendor and the conveyancing lawyer is handling it, the customary fee for drawing such a mortgage is one-third of the tariff. Fees on agreements for sale are calculated on the full purchase price of the property. The standard fee for clearing title is between $60 and $90 per mortgage to be cleared, plus disbursements.

Keep in mind that lawyers' fees for many legal services can vary. However, remember that price should not be the only consideration in selecting a lawyer. The quality of the work, the service given, and the competence of the supervising lawyer in real estate matters should also be weighed. The person who uses price as the only criterion may end up getting only a cut-rate job.

To briefly summarize then, a conveyance by itself is not too expensive, but, when combined with other documents such as mortgages, the lawyer's fees plus disbursements can escalate quite rapidly.

In the usual type of house conveyance transaction, it is usual for the purchaser's lawyer doing the conveyance also to look after clearing the title. Although normally the same lawyer should not be acting for both parties, it is accepted practice in a normal type of real estate transaction, since the possibilities of the lawyer having a conflict of interest between the two parties is not too great and also because the purchase funds are commonly used to discharge the vendor's mortgages. However, in situations where there could be, or there arises, a dispute or conflict of interest between the vendor and the purchaser, the vendor should seek independent legal advice immediately.

If a lawyer charges what the client feels is an unreasonable fee, the client has the option of having the lawyer's bill "taxed." Basically this involves submitting an application to the court so that a hearing will be set up before the court registrar, who will then review the lawyer's account and determine whether or not the bill is fair.

To get started, simply go down to your nearest courthouse and ask to see the registrar. It is important to note that if a client wishes to have a lawyer's bill taxed, application for a taxation must be made within one year of the date the account is rendered or the registrar may refuse to grant the taxation.

It is interesting to note that if you have a lawyer's bill taxed, the court registrar may use, as a guideline, the Supreme Court tariff which usually is lower than what a lawyer's standard charge is. However, where there is a prior agreement setting the fee in advance, such agreement would govern.

A client may negotiate the fee in advance with the lawyer. Sometimes it is difficult for a lawyer to determine the exact fee at the beginning of the transaction, not being certain at that point of all the difficulties that may be encountered. The lawyer should, however, be able to estimate the figure, depending upon the complexity of the matter. There is no need to feel embarrassed about asking for a quote from a lawyer so that you can properly organize your financial affairs. By doing this, the transaction may be closed as soon as possible and there will be no misunderstandings later on.

d. THE CONVEYANCE (OR TRANSFER OF TITLE)

1. Instructions to the lawyer

Ideally, you should consult a lawyer *before* signing the interim agreement so that you can get assistance in drafting the terms of the offer. If, however, as is usually the case, you did not contact your lawyer until after signing the interim agreement, you should submit a copy of the agreement so that the lawyer can become familiar with all the terms of the sale and other important information.

If a mortgage is to be arranged, a lawyer will also need to know who is providing the mortgage money and, if possible, which lawyer will act on behalf of the lender, so that registration of the mortgage and the deed can be coordinated.

By knowing the address or legal description of the property, the lawyer can arrange to have the property searched in the Land Title Office and order tax certificates.

The real estate sales agent will also be contacted and requested to provide a sales report. This sales report includes a copy of the interim agreement, a summary of the transaction, the name of the vendor and the vendor's lawyer (if any), and any other pertinent information about the transaction.

2. In whose name should the property be registered?

If a person is married, various considerations influence the decision as to how title is to be registered. Although there may be good business reasons (protecting the property from business claims against one spouse) for registering the property in the name of one spouse only, most married couples want the title registered in the name of both spouses, as they feel the home is jointly theirs. These factors are discussed in more detail a bit further on in this section.

The two most common methods of multiple ownership are joint tenancy and tenancy in common. In each of these types of ownership, each spouse is the sole owner of an undivided half interest in the whole of the property. Thus, the two spouses' interests comprise the whole of the ownership of the property. That is, neither spouse is able to draw a physical line through the property and lay claim to one half or the other.

The difference between joint tenancy and tenancy in common is that a joint tenancy has the right of survivorship associated with it. This means that, if one spouse dies, the other automatically becomes entitled to the other half of the property.

191

If one spouse dies in a tenancy in common, that spouse's interest passes to the estate and is distributed according to the terms of the will, which may or may not mean that the surviving spouse will get it.

It is important to note that, in order to create a joint tenancy, all owners must take their interest in the property at the same time and all owners must also own equal shares of the property. It is not possible for the husband to hold a six-tenths interest in the property and the wife a four-tenths interest and still hold such interest as joint tenants. (Please note that marriage is not a prerequisite to holding property as joint tenants. Any two or more people can hold property either as joint tenants or tenants in common.)

Before automatically registering the property in joint ownership, the following questions should be considered:

(a) Who will supply the money for the down payment?

(b) Who will be primarily responsible for the payment of the mortgage?

(c) What is the likelihood of the marriage being successful?

(d) What is the exposure to liability of each of the parties?

(e) What will be the income tax brackets of the individuals after purchase?

The spouse contributing the money to a joint purchase is usually presumed to have made a gift to the other spouse. Therefore, should the marriage fail, that spouse cannot later claim ownership of the property on the basis that his or her money was used to purchase the property.

Therefore, the likelihood of the marriage being successful is a factor to be given serious consideration. If there is any doubt as to its success, it is foolish for the contributing partner to either become excluded from or give up part of the ownership; once it is gone it can be very difficult, if at all possible, to retrieve. Even if the home is registered in the name of the husband alone, the wife may, if there are marital difficulties, obtain part ownership through the Family Relations Act or apply under the Land (Wife Protection) Act to register a lien against the home, thus preventing the husband from selling the home until the wife either voluntarily gives up and discharges the lien, moves away from the home, or dies. This applies equally, by the way, to a husband where the property is registered in the wife's name only.

The exposure to liability of each of the parties is also very important. For example, if a couple has a successful marriage and each has contributed an equal amount of money to the purchase, it may seem logical to register the property in joint tenancy. However, if the husband is in a very risky business, this factor alone could dictate that the property should be registered in the wife's name only and that payments toward the home should be made by the husband as a gift. In this manner, the equity in the home would be protected from the business creditors of the husband.

The decision about how the title is to be registered does not necessarily have to be made prior to signing the interim agreement. This can, in most instances, be changed with the permission of the vendor prior to the completion of the transaction.

3. Survey certificate

Just as a mortgage company may want a survey certificate to ascertain that there are no encroachments, easements, or rights-of-way affecting security, the prudent purchaser should also make sure that one is obtained.

This is something the lawyer normally will not automatically do unless requested. However, if a survey certificate is obtained, the lawyer will examine it for you. In many instances it is possible for the lawyer to submit a copy of the survey to the municipality in which the property is located so that it can tell you if the information shown on the survey complies with the relevant bylaws of the municipality.

4. Title search

After receiving instructions on the conveyance or on the mortgage from the mortgage company, a lawyer will, first of all, search the title of the property. These searches are done in the Land Title Office for the appropriate jurisdiction in which the land is situated.

British Columbia is divided into seven land registration districts, encompassing the entire province. The seven districts are known as the Kamloops, Nelson, New Westminster, Prince George, Prince Rupert, Vancouver, and Victoria land registration districts.

The Land Title Office for each district is located in the city by which the land registry is known. It is possible to obtain a map of the land registration districts from the nearest government agent. Normally, land located in the vicinity of a particular land registration district bearing its name falls within the jurisdiction of that land registration district.

However, the boundaries between the Vancouver and the New Westminster land registration districts sometimes cause problems. Land located in Richmond, Delta, Surrey, Burnaby, New Westminster, and the rest of the Fraser Valley is located in the New Westminster land registration district. Land located in Vancouver, North and West Vancouver, and the Sunshine Coast is located in the Vancouver land registration district. The Gulf Islands and Vancouver Island are located in the Victoria land registration district.

British Columbia has a Torrens registration system of land titles. The most obvious advantage of the Torrens system is that the title to land can be verified by a simple procedure in the appropriate Land Title Office. It is not necessary to conduct a detailed search of title, tracing the entire dealings with the subject property back to the original grant from the

Crown, as it would be in a jurisdiction where the Torrens system is not in use, or to insure the title with a title insurance company as is done in most parts of the United States.

Thus, by doing a search of the latest title on the property in question you can determine who the owners are and what charges and encumbrances are registered against the title. Section 38(1) of the Land Title Act provides, subject to the exceptions set out, that such title can be relied on by both the owner and any other person dealing with that owner.

It does not matter whether fraud has been practised by the registered owner in obtaining the title, as long as the person to whom it is sold has no knowledge of the fraud. The person who purchases with no knowledge of the fraud will obtain an absolutely safe title which cannot be challenged or upset by an innocent party who was fraudulently done out of the property.

When you buy legal title to a property, you submit a title transfer document to the appropriate Land Title Office. This document is really an application to have the certificate of title transferred to the new owner. The registrar of titles, if everything is in order, will then register the application by creating or issuing a new certificate of title and cancelling the old one.

If the person making the application is claiming some interest less than the entire interest or fee simple in the property (that is, a charge such as a mortgage, agreement for sale, easement, or building scheme) and if the registrar finds everything in order, the charge claimed will be registered by endorsing a notation on the certificate of title.

The Land Title Act also provides that the document that is not registered has no effect against the people whose documents are registered. This is important.

Take, for example, the previous illustration of Penny McScrooge and Fast Eddie O'Greedy. When Penny bought the property from Fast Eddie, Fast Eddie provided Penny with a title transfer document and Penny paid the purchase price. If Penny had left her document for a couple of days before taking it down to the Land Title Office, Fast Eddie, who did not appear to be the most honest person, could have sold (or further mortgaged) his property to Johnny Kumlately, who could have registered his interest immediately.

As Johnny's documents would have been registered prior to Penny's, he would have been recognized as having title to the property. Penny would have been unable to register her documents and, therefore, her documents and her interest would not have been recognized. Her only remedy would have been to sue Fast Eddie for damages for fraud.

As you can see, it is vital for the protection of your property interest that the document evidencing the interest be registered as soon as possible after you have received the interest in the property. It is also important for you to be able to double-check that such interest has been registered before paying over any funds.

A search of the title will normally be done three times. The first time the search of the title is made is after instructions are received. Photocopies of the title and all charges and relevant plans affecting the property should also be obtained. This search is used for the preparation of the documents.

The second search is called the pre-registration search. This is made immediately before the documents are submitted for registration and it is merely an updating of the initial search to make sure that nothing has changed.

The third search is called the post-registration search and is usually done first thing the day after the documents have been submitted for registration. It is only after this search checks out that money should be paid over to the vendor.

The first search received by the lawyer will consist of a search of the "index," a search of the title, together with an abstract or photocopy of the title, photocopies of all encumbrances (e.g., rights-of-way of mortgages), photocopies of any relevant judgments, and photocopies of the relevant parts of the subdivision plan.

If the property being searched is a strata lot, the strata plan should also be searched for any changes or amendments to the bylaws.

These documents are then reviewed thoroughly by the lawyer to ascertain whether or not the vendor is going to have any difficulties delivering what he or she has contracted to do in the interim agreement. This, depending on the terms of the transaction, may include checking the mortgage document to see if it can be assumed or discharged.

The purchaser, if assuming any encumbrances, will have to comply with the conditions set out in those encumbrances, and, therefore, right-of-way agreements, land-use contracts, building schemes, etc., should be reviewed carefully to make sure that the house complies with the conditions set out and/or that the purchaser is prepared to comply with such conditions if necessary. Some of the most common of these will be discussed briefly.

Many properties are subject to an easement in favor of the local municipality, hydro, or telephone company. These easements are usually located along the rear or the side boundary of the property and are usually one to three metres wide.

The purpose of the easements is to allow the municipality, hydro, or telephone company to enter the property to install lines of service and, subsequently, to repair, operate, or maintain these lines of service.

The standard form of this type of easement usually contains a clause by the party wanting the easement to repair or restore the surface of the land if the land is disturbed. It should be noted, however, that most easements or rights-of-way cannot be built upon and should be kept relatively clear of obstructions.

Building schemes are really restrictive covenants. A restrictive covenant is a promise by one landowner to another not to do certain things with the property. A restrictive covenant may, by its terms, be binding upon subsequent purchasers of the land. For example, a restrictive covenant may provide that the plans and specifications of any building to be built on the land must receive the approval of the subdivider of the land. This type of restrictive covenant attempts to ensure that a certain quality of housing will be maintained in the specified area.

If the search reveals that any mechanics' liens, judgments against the vendor (or purchaser), caveats, or *lis pendens* have been filed, arrangements should be made to have these cleared before proceeding with registration or paying any funds to the vendor.

In addition to the land title searches, a search will also be done at the office of the municipality (or other applicable taxing authority) as to whether the real property and utility taxes have been paid.

Where a strata lot is being conveyed, an additional search and appropriate certificates should be obtained from the strata council with respect to the monthly contributions. (This was discussed in detail in chapter 7.)

5. Conveyancing documentation

Certain conveyancing documentation is prepared only because it is a requirement of the Land Title Office. Form A — Freehold Transfer, citizenship declarations, and the property transfer tax form fall into this category.

Other conveyancing documentation is prepared for the benefit of the vendor or purchaser and has no relevance as far as the Land Title Office is concerned. The Statement of Adjustments and personal agreements between the vendor and the purchaser fall into this category.

Finally, the title transfer document, agreement for sale or mortgage, discharge of mortgage, etc. are prepared for the mutual benefit of the Land Title Office and the vendor, purchaser, and/or lender.

The property transfer tax form — or FIN579 — (see Sample #8) serves three main purposes. First, it is used to calculate the property transfer tax to be collected by the Land Title Office. Second, it provides the assessment authority with notice of a change of ownership so that the tax records of the owners can be amended accordingly. Third, it provides the assessment authorities with an indication of the market price of the property for property tax assessment purposes.

A citizenship declaration is a requirement of the provincial government. Its only purpose is to provide the government with information about the citizenship of land owners. Although the declaration may be the first step, there is currently no prohibition against, or additional taxes on, non-citizens owning land. However, unless a citizenship declaration accompanies the application to have the ownership of the land (whether legal or beneficial) transferred, the application will not be accepted.

It has now become the practice to include in the Statement of Adjustments covenants amounting to a supplemental agreement between the vendor and purchaser wherein the parties can obtain the additional covenants that they require. This should be provided for in the interim agreement and care should be taken that it has been inserted.

An example of a covenant is the promise of the vendor to indemnify the purchaser against any claim that the purchaser may be liable for under section 116 of the Income Tax Act if the vendor is a non-resident for Canadian income tax purposes and, also, the representation that the vendor is not a non-resident.

SAMPLE #8
PROPERTY TRANSFER TAX RETURN

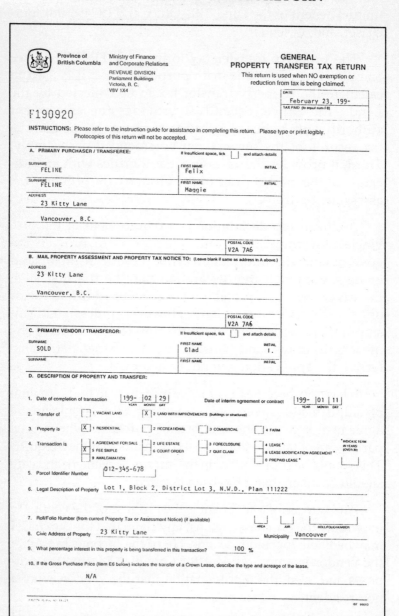

Province of British Columbia

Ministry of Finance and Corporate Relations
REVENUE DIVISION
Parliament Buildings
Victoria, B. C.
V8V 1X4

GENERAL
PROPERTY TRANSFER TAX RETURN
This return is used when NO exemption or reduction from tax is being claimed.

DATE
February 23, 199-
TAX PAID (to equal item F8)

F190920

INSTRUCTIONS: Please refer to the instruction guide for assistance in completing this return. Please type or print legibly. Photocopies of this return will not be accepted.

A. PRIMARY PURCHASER / TRANSFEREE: If insufficient space, tick [ ] and attach details

SURNAME FELINE   FIRST NAME Felix   INITIAL

SURNAME FELINE   FIRST NAME Maggie   INITIAL

ADDRESS
23 Kitty Lane

Vancouver, B.C.

POSTAL CODE
V2A 7A6

B. MAIL PROPERTY ASSESSMENT AND PROPERTY TAX NOTICE TO: (Leave blank if same as address in A above.)

ADDRESS
23 Kitty Lane

Vancouver, B.C.

POSTAL CODE
V2A 7A6

C. PRIMARY VENDOR / TRANSFEROR: If insufficient space, tick [ ] and attach details

SURNAME SOLD   FIRST NAME Glad   INITIAL I.

SURNAME   FIRST NAME   INITIAL

D. DESCRIPTION OF PROPERTY AND TRANSFER:

1. Date of completion of transaction   199- | 02 | 29 | Date of interim agreement or contract   199- | 01 | 11 |
   YEAR MONTH DAY   YEAR MONTH DAY

2. Transfer of   [ ] 1 VACANT LAND   [X] 2 LAND WITH IMPROVEMENTS (buildings or structures)

3. Property is   [X] 1 RESIDENTIAL   [ ] 2 RECREATIONAL   [ ] 3 COMMERCIAL   [ ] 4 FARM

4. Transaction is   [ ] 1 AGREEMENT FOR SALE [ ] 2 LIFE ESTATE [ ] 3 FORECLOSURE [ ] 4 LEASE *   * INDICATE TERM IN YEARS (OVER 30)
   [X] 5 FEE SIMPLE [ ] 6 COURT ORDER [ ] 7 QUIT CLAIM [ ] 8 LEASE MODIFICATION AGREEMENT *
   [ ] 9 AMALGAMATION   [ ] 0 PREPAID LEASE *

5. Parcel Identifier Number   012-345-678

6. Legal Description of Property   Lot 1, Block 2, District Lot 3, N.W.D., Plan 111222

7. Roll/Folio Number (from current Property Tax or Assessment Notice) (if available)   [AREA] [AJR] [ROLL/FOLIO NUMBER]

8. Civic Address of Property   23 Kitty Lane   Municipality Vancouver

9. What percentage interest in this property is being transferred in this transaction?   100 %

10. If the Gross Purchase Price (Item E6 below) includes the transfer of a Crown Lease, describe the type and acreage of the lease.

   N/A

200

- 2 -

E. TERMS:

	AMORTIZATION PERIOD (MONTHS)	RENEWAL TERM (MONTHS)	INTEREST RATE (%/ANNUM)	PRINCIPAL AMOUNT			
1. Cash					$ 45,051 00	E1
2. Financing						
a. New - first						
b. New - second	36		12 00	25,000 00		
c. Assumed	36		10 00	119,949 00	TOTAL OF ITEMS 2a THRU 2d	
d. Agreement for sale					144,949 00	E2
3. Forgiveness of debt						E3
4. Property taken in trade						E4
5. Other consideration paid or given (details)						E5
6. GROSS PURCHASE PRICE (TOTAL OF E1, E2, E3, E4 AND E5 ABOVE)					$ 190,000 00	E6

F. PROPERTY TRANSFER TAX CALCULATION:

1. Fair market value of property or interest in property	$ 190,000 00	F1
4. 1% on first $200,000 of taxable amount (F1)	1,900 00	F4
5. 2% on remainder of taxable amount (F1)	--	F5
8. PROPERTY TRANSFER TAX PAYABLE (F4 plus F5)	1,900 00	F8

H. ALLOCATION OF GROSS PURCHASE PRICE (NON-RESIDENTIAL PROPERTIES ONLY):

1. Real property (land and buildings)	$ 189,500 00	H1
2. Machinery, furniture, and equipment		H2
3. Fixtures (as defined under the *Social Service Tax Act*)	500 00	H3
4. Goodwill, quotas and other intangibles		H4
5. Other - describe _____		H5
6. GROSS PURCHASE PRICE (TOTAL OF H1 THRU H5 TO EQUAL E6)	$ 190,000 00	H6

NOTE: Tax is payable under the *Social Service Tax Act* on the purchase of machinery, furniture and equipment (H2 above) and fixtures (H3 above)

I. ADDITIONAL INFORMATION:

3. If the gross purchase price (E6) differs from the fair market value (F1), indicate the reason for the difference

☐ 1 CONVEYANCE ONLY	☐ 2 RELATED PARTY	☐ 3 SPECIAL INTEREST	☐ 4 DISTRESS SALE	☐ 5 FORECLOSURE
☐ 6 SALE OF PART INTEREST	☐ 7 TRADE	☐ OTHER		

4. If the terms of this transaction includes property taken in trade (E4), identify the property by providing

AREA	JUR	ROLL/FOLIO NUMBER	LEGAL DESCRIPTION

PARCEL IDENTIFIER   ADDRESS

CERTIFICATION – The undersigned hereby certifies that the information given is complete and correct in all respects.

SIGNATURE *Felix Feline*	SIGNATURE *Maggie Feline*
NAME Felix Feline	NAME Maggie Feline
ADDRESS 23 Kitty Lane	ADDRESS 23 Kitty Lane
Vancouver, B.C. V2A 7A6	Vancouver, B.C. V2A 7A6
PHONE NO. 234-5678	PHONE NO. 234-5678

FIN 579 - G Rev. 92 / 11 / 23

Other covenants may be that no person other than the vendor is entitled to claim an interest in the lands under the Family Relations Act, that there are no monies owing to the strata corporation, that all buildings and improvements conform with municipal and civic bylaws relating to the lands, that the vendor has done no other acts to encumber the lands except as disclosed, that the buildings and improvements do not encroach on other lands, and that all taxes and other such charges have been paid except as otherwise disclosed in the Statement of Adjustments.

Besides the property transfer tax return and citizenship declaration, the Land Title Office requires a Form A — Freehold Transfer, the title transfer document. The purpose of this document is simply to evidence the transfer of the property from the vendor to the purchaser (see Sample #9). It contains no covenants, warranties, or representations as it did prior to the revision of the Land Title Act.

A common covenant then would have been for the purchaser to assume the vendor's mortgage and comply with all its terms and conditions and indemnify and save the vendor harmless from any claim under its terms. This covenant has now been statutorily imposed on the purchaser in section 20 of the Property and Law Act when the purchaser assumes title subject to a mortgage, unless otherwise expressly indicated.

The Statement of Adjustments is the document recording the accounting of the real estate transaction between the vendor and the purchaser. It is customary for the purchaser's lawyer to draw both a vendor's and a purchaser's Statement of Adjustments. An example of each has been reproduced in Samples #10 and #11.

As you can see, the Statement of Adjustments merely allocates and adjusts the expenses between the vendor and purchaser. All expenses in connection with the house up to the adjustment date are the responsibility of the vendor. If the purchaser actually pays for any such expenses later (i.e., taxes

SAMPLE #9
FREEHOLD TRANSFER

6.01

LAND TITLE ACT
FORM A
(Section 181 (1))

**Province of
British Columbia**

FREEHOLD TRANSFER (This area for Land Title Office use) PAGE 1 of _____ pages

1. APPLICATION: (Name, address, phone number and signature of applicant, applicant's solicitor or agent)

Diane Lawyer of Best & Knowitall, Barristers & Solicitors,
1234 - 5th Street, Vancouver, B.C. V1A 3Z2   681-0123

2. (a) PARCEL IDENTIFIER AND LEGAL DESCRIPTION OF LAND:*
(PID)   (LEGAL DESCRIPTION)

012 345 678   Lot 1, Block 2, Group 3, N.W.D., Plan 111222

(b) MARKET VALUE: $ 190 000.00

3. CONSIDERATION: $1.00 and other good and valuable consideration

4. TRANSFEROR(S):*   Glad I. Sold

5. FREEHOLD ESTATE TRANSFERRED:* Fee Simple

6. TRANSFEREE(S): (including occupation(s), postal address(es) and postal code(s)) *

FELIX FELINE, Veterinarian, and
MAGGIE FELINE, Nurse, both of
23 Kitty Lane, Vancouver,
British Columbia, V2A 7A6

7. EXECUTION(S):** The transferor(s) accept(s) the above consideration and understand(s) that this instrument operates to transfer the freehold estate in the land described above to the transferee(s).

| Officer Signature(s) | Execution Date | | | Transferor(s) Signature(s) |
	Y	M	D	
John R. Barrister	9–	04	20	*Glad I. Sold*
JOHN R. BARRISTER				GLAD I. SOLD
Solicitor				
17 Court Case Lane				
Victoria, B.C.				
321-1567				

OFFICER CERTIFICATION:
Your signature constitutes a representation that you are a solicitor, notary public or other person authorized by the *Evidence Act*, R.S.B.C. 1979, c. 116, to take affidavits for use in British Columbia and certifies the matters set out in Part 5 of the *Land Title Act* as they pertain to the execution of this instrument.

*   If space insufficient, enter "SEE SCHEDULE" and attach schedule in Form E.
** If space insufficient, continue executions on additional page(s) in Form D.

SAMPLE #10
VENDOR'S STATEMENT

VENDOR'S STATEMENT OF ADJUSTMENTS

VENDOR:	Glad I. Sold
PURCHASER:	Felix Feline and Maggie Feline
LEGAL DESCRIPTION:	Lot 1, Block 2, District Lot 345, Group 1, Plan 111222
CIVIC ADDRESS:	23 Kitty Lane, Vancouver, B.C.
ADJUSTMENT DATE:	March 1, 199-
POSSESSION DATE:	March 1, 199-
COMPLETION DATE:	February 29, 199-

	DEBIT	CREDIT
TO SELLING PRICE:		$ 190,000.00
BY TAX ADJUSTMENT ADJUSTED NET - (taxes to be paid by Purchaser) 2/12($1,580 - $380)	$ 200.00	
TO WATER ADJUSTMENT (Already paid by Vendor) 10/12 x $45.00		37.50
BY COMMISSION PAYABLE TO SLOTH REALTY LTD.	3,000.00	
BY ASSUMPTION OF FIRST MORTGAGE IN FAVOUR OF XYZ TRUST COMPANY Balance at February 1, 199- after payment by Vendor $119,049.89 BY ACCRUED INTEREST TO ADJUSTMENT DATE 899.11 $119,949.00	119,949.00	
BY AMOUNT GRANTED BY VENDOR TO PURCHASER AS SECOND MORTGAGE	25,000.00	
BY BALANCE PAYABLE TO VENDOR ON COMPLETION	41,888.50	
	$ 190,037.50	$ 190,037.50

Approved by the Vendor this 25th day of February, 199- .

GLAD I. SOLD

*Items that begin with "to" are credits to the Vendor.
**Items that begin with "by" are debits to the Vendor.

204

NOTES:

1.   All other adjustments customarily made such as fuel, hydro, and telephone to be settled directly between the parties at the time of possession.

2.   Purchaser to place fire insurance effective as of completion date.

3.   Purchaser to make March 1, 199- , mortgage payment in the amount of $1,250.00 to XYZ Trust Company.

4.   Purchase price includes a refrigerator and stove valued at $500.00 and the Purchaser shall remit Sales Tax on the same.

5.   The Vendor is to deliver vacant possession of the property being purchased on or before the possession date.

6.   The Vendor authorizes and directs the Purchaser's solicitor to pay the balance of the real estate commission to Sloth Realty Ltd.

7.   The Vendor is responsible for all costs, expenses and interest charges in connection with clearing the encumbrances to be cleared, if any, as set out in the Statement of Adjustments.

8.   The Vendor is to terminate any automatic repayment for encumbrances being discharged directly.

9.   The Vendor represents and warrants that he is not a "non-resident" as defined in the Income Tax Act of Canada and agrees to indemnify and save harmless the Purchaser for any claims or costs arising out of any tax liability of a "non-resident".

10.   The Vendor agrees that all representations, covenants and agreements set out in the Interim Agreement executed by the Vendor and Purchaser preceding this transaction shall not merge upon the execution and registration of the conveyancing documents.

11.   The Vendor hereby authorizes Diane Lawyer as solicitor for the Purchasers to disburse the funds in the manner set out herein and further confirms that all figures are correct. The Vendor further acknowledges that Diane Lawyer acts as solicitor for the Purchasers only in connection with this real estate transaction and does not represent the Vendor except only to the extent that the Vendor wishes Diane Lawyer to retire or pay any mortgage or other indebtedness being paid from the sale proceeds. The Vendor further is advised to consult a solicitor or other advisor of his choice with respect to all matters in connection with this transaction, especially if the Vendor does not fully understand or approve of any aspect herein.

Approved and consented to:

GLAD I. SOLD

PURCHASER'S STATEMENT

PURCHASER'S STATEMENT OF ADJUSTMENTS

		DEBIT	CREDIT
VENDOR:	Glad I. Sold		
PURCHASER:	Felix Feline and Maggie Feline		
LEGAL DESCRIPTION:	Lot 1, Block 2, District Lot 345, Group 1, Plan 111222		
CIVIC ADDRESS:	23 Kitty Lane, Vancouver, B.C.		
ADJUSTMENT DATE:	March 1, 199-		
POSSESSION DATE:	March 1, 199-		
COMPLETION DATE:	February 29, 199-		

	DEBIT	CREDIT
BY SELLING PRICE:	$ 190,000.00	
TO TAX ADJUSTMENT ADJUSTED NET - (taxes to be paid by Purchaser) 2/12($1,580 - $380)		$ 200.00
TO WATER ADJUSTMENT (Already paid by Vendor) 10/12 x $45.00	37.50	
TO DEPOSIT PAID TO SLOTH REALTY LTD.		1,000.00
TO ASSUMPTION OF FIRST MORTGAGE IN FAVOUR OF XYZ TRUST COMPANY Balance at February 1, 199- after payment by Vendor $119,049.89 BY ACCRUED INTEREST TO ADJUSTMENT DATE 899.11 $119,949.00		119,949.00
TO AMOUNT GRANTED BY VENDOR TO PURCHASERS AS SECOND MORTGAGE		25,000.00
BY SOLICITOR'S FEE FOR CONVEYANCE AND SECOND MORTGAGE	587.50	
BY DISBURSEMENTS INCURRED BY SOLICITOR IN CONNECTION WITH THE CONVEYANCE	143.50	
BY PROPERTY PURCHASE TAX	1,900.00	
TO BALANCE PAYABLE BY PURCHASERS ON COMPLETION		46,519.50
	$ 192,668.50	$ 192,668.50

Approved by the Purchasers this 26th day of February, 199- .

Felix Felin
— FELIX FELINE —

Maggie Feline
MAGGIE FELINE

*Items that begin with "by" are debits to the Purchaser.
**Items that begin with "to" are credits to the Purchaser.

NOTES:

1.   All other adjustments customarily made such as fuel, hydro, and telephone to be settled directly between the parties at the time of possession.

2.   Purchaser to place fire insurance effective as of completion date.

3.   Purchaser to make March 1, 199- , mortgage payment in the amount of $1,250.00 to XYZ Trust Company.

4.   Purchase price includes a refrigerator and stove having a total value of $500.00 and the Purchaser is aware that Sales Tax should be paid with respect to such and/or any other chattels being conveyed by the Vendor to the Purchaser.

5.   The Vendor is to deliver vacant possession of the property being purchased on or before the possession date.

6.   The Purchaser authorizes Diane Lawyer to disburse funds upon acceptance of the conveyancing documents for filing in the Land Title Office and conducting a satisfactory post registration index search.

7.   It is the responsibility of the Purchaser to investigate setback requirements. The Purchaser has been advised that a survey should be obtained if a recent survey is not available.

8.   In the event that there have been recent improvements made to the structure or appurtenances placed on the property, the Purchaser is aware of the possibility of a Builders Lien being filed against the property. In the event that the structure is being purchased from an owner/contractor, the Purchaser has been advised that if Builders Liens are filed within the prescribed time (30 days after substantial completion), and if such liens are found to be valid, such liens would attach to the interest of the Purchaser in the building and the holdback provisions, as set out in the Builders Lien Act will not protect the Purchaser unless the holdback is sufficient to satisfy the entire amount of the liens.

9.   Title is being acquired by the Purchaser subject to reservations in favour of the Crown and the mortgage in favour of XYZ Trust Company. There are no existing easements, rights-of-way, and restrictive covenants.

10.   It is the responsibility of the Purchaser to verify zoning, occupancy permit, building permit, availability of business licenses, Health and Fire Department deficiencies.

11.   It is the responsibility of the Purchaser to satisfy himself as to any faulty equipment on the premises, or structural deficiencies to the building.

Approved and consented to:

_____
FELIX FELINE

_____
MAGGIE FELINE

which are usually paid for the whole year in July or August depending on the municipality) the purchaser should receive a credit for the vendor's share of such expenses in the Statement of Adjustments.

Likewise, if the vendor has already prepaid expenses in connection with the house, the purchaser should reimburse the vendor for such expenses in the Statement of Adjustments.

In order to properly prepare the Statement of Adjustments shown in our example, the conveyancing lawyer has to obtain the assumption figure from XYZ Trust Company. The total commission and the amount of the deposit is obtained from the sales record sheet forwarded by the real estate agent. The tax adjustment information is obtained from the tax office of the municipality in question.

Thus, in this transaction, where taxes will become due and be payable in July of 199- for the whole calendar year (i.e., January 1, 199- to December 31, 199-) and the payment of such taxes will be the responsibility of the purchaser, the purchaser is reimbursed for two months of his net taxes since the adjustment date is March 1.

Since the seller is responsible for the first two months of the year's taxes, he should reimburse the purchaser for January and February. Since the purchaser can claim the homeowner's grant of $380 (under 65) the adjustment is done on a net basis. Likewise, the vendor is reimbursed for water that had been prepaid on behalf of the purchaser.

The remaining part of the Statement of Adjustments is fairly self-explanatory. Items like fuel, hydro, and telephone are normally not included on the Statement of Adjustments because it is customary for the parties to notify the hydro authorities so that a reading can be made at the appropriate time and the hydro records changed. The same goes for the telephone. In the instances where the house is heated with oil, arrangements should also be made to have the tank dipped and tested for water content. This will be done free of charge by the fuel supplier. The purchaser should then reimburse the vendor for the amount of oil that is in the tank prior to the purchaser's occupancy.

6. Closing the transaction

The date that the transaction is to close (completion date) is set out in the interim agreement. By that date all the conveyancing documentation should have been completed and signed by both the vendor and the purchaser. The purchaser's money should also have been paid to the lawyer, who would hold it in trust.

On closing the deal, the purchaser's lawyer is concerned with three areas of the transaction — title, possession, and proper accounting for the funds paid by the purchaser.

With regard to title, the purchaser's lawyer's job is to ensure that the purchaser has obtained the title that the vendor agreed to sell in the interim agreement, subject to any deficiencies that the purchaser may subsequently (but prior to closing) authorize and accept.

The purchaser's lawyer, knowing what the status of the title was when the first search was done and knowing what it should look like after the purchase has been completed, will do a pre-registration search prior to submitting the documents for registration.

As previously mentioned, the purpose of the pre-registration search is to make sure that nothing has changed from the original search. The documents are then submitted and a post-registration search is done the following morning in order to allow all registrations of that day to be posted on the "index." If this time period were not allowed, it could conceivably be possible for a judgment against the vendor to be registered immediately and the purchaser's property would then be subject to the judgment.

With regard to possession, the purchaser should be able to enter into occupancy on the possession date as specified in the interim agreement. The transfer of a key from the vendor to the purchaser is the usual manner in which a change of possession is made. In most circumstances the key is transferred either through arrangements with the real estate agent, the lawyer, or between the parties themselves.

As far as accounting between the parties goes, the purchaser's lawyer will want to make sure that there is enough money in trust to pay the vendor and the other various parties that need to be paid out according to the vendor's Statement of Adjustments.

Therefore, the purchaser will be requested to supply a certified cheque for the amount due, as shown in the Statement of Adjustments. The purchaser's lawyer should also have verified that the vendor has in actual fact paid for the various items for which credit has been given on the Statement of Adjustments.

In the past, the closing of a real estate transaction was a ceremonious affair. However, today in British Columbia, most real estate transactions are closed without the vendor or purchaser meeting each other. After the documentation has been prepared and signed by the parties, the purchaser's lawyer will take care of the registration. After checking the post-registration search and making sure that everything is normal, the lawyer will then pay out the money according to the Statement of Adjustments or order to pay. The lawyer will then send the purchaser a reporting letter.

7. Solicitor's report

Although there is no set format for a solicitor's report, the following areas should be covered in the report to the purchaser:

(a) The registration particulars of the documents filed in the Land Title Office complete with numbers and dates

(b) A professional opinion on the title

(c) Copies of all conveyancing documents such as transfer forms, vendor and purchaser agreements, mortgages, and statements of adjustments not previously supplied to the purchaser. These would also include copies of encumbrances that the purchaser would be assuming, as well as a copy of the relevant portion of the plan showing the property outline. (All these documents should, of course, have been previously discussed and reviewed with the purchaser.)

(d) An accounting between the lawyer and the purchaser as to the disposal of the purchaser's funds. This is usually done either in the letter itself or by attaching a statement of trust funds showing the receipt and disbursement of funds through the lawyer's trust account. Also, the lawyer will usually, at this time, submit a bill and take the amount due out of the money held in trust. This will show up in the purchaser's Statement of Adjustments.

In the reporting letter, the lawyer will usually mention having ordered a State of Title Certificate, which is issued by the Land Title Office and certifies the status of the title as of a certain time and date. Many lawyers will order the certificate and forward it to their client either in support of their own opinion or as a basis of their opinion.

8.   Dealings with old mortgages

If the vendor has, in the interim agreement, agreed to deliver clear title, it is the vendor's responsibility to have any existing mortgage discharged from the title on or before closing. A vendor cannot legally require a purchaser to complete a real estate transaction unless the mortgage is discharged.

If a purchaser strictly wishes to insist on the legal right, a problem is created where the vendor requires a portion of the purchaser price to be paid to satisfy the old mortgage account. This problem can usually be resolved in one of the following ways:

(a) The vendor will have to supply money on an interim basis to pay off the existing mortgage and provide clear title. As this method, in many instances, could put a heavy onus on the vendor, it is not used often.

(b) The vendor (or the purchaser's lawyer who will in most instances be acting on behalf of the vendor in clearing the title to the property) will make arrangements with the lender to have a discharge of the mortgage prepared and available for the closing, provided the purchaser's lawyer undertakes to pay to the lender the balance due under the mortgage. This is a more satisfactory arrangement, as the purchaser will, on closing, receive title to the property clear of the mortgage. However, many lenders, particularly institutional lenders, will refuse to prepare a discharge of the outstanding amount of the mortgage. Therefore, with institutional investors, the following alternative (c) could be used.

(c) The vendor and the purchaser agree that the transaction will be completed on the understanding that the mortgage will be discharged after the closing of the transaction. In this instance, the purchaser's lawyer will obtain an undertaking from the mortgage company to provide a discharge of the mortgage upon payment to it of the balance of the mortgage money and, when the discharge is received, it is then filed for registration. It should be noted that, because of the time gap involved, there is an element of risk. This method should not be used if the lender is an individual or a smaller company because of the risk of not receiving it.

If the purchaser is assuming the vendor's mortgage, the purchaser or the purchaser's lawyer should obtain confirmation of the following items from the lender:

(a) The balance that will be owing under the mortgage as of the date closing

(b) That the terms of the mortgage are set out in the documents registered in the Land Title Office and have not been amended or altered in any way

(c) That there are no outstanding matters between the vendor and the lender that would be detrimental to the assumption of the mortgage by the purchaser

9. Is the property being rented?

If all or part of the property being sold is rented, the following matters should be checked. First, you should check the zoning to make sure that it permits revenue suites. (The lawyer will in most instances not check this unless requested. The lawyer's primary concern is with the status of the title.) If it doesn't, check with municipal authorities to determine their attitude regarding "illegal" suites and then take a chance that they will not reverse their stand. This is not a problem if the complete house is rented to one tenant or that tenant's immediate family.

Second, the purchaser should be satisfied that the terms of the tenancy are listed properly in the interim agreement. The terms and conditions of tenancy should be confirmed by the tenants prior to closing. Not only should the amount of rent be covered but also the term of the tenancy, the amount of the damage deposit (if any), prepaid rent, whether or not there is an unregistered lease, and any additional services to be supplied under the tenancy.

Third, it should be remembered that prepaid rent and damage deposits may need to be adjusted in the Statement of Adjustments.

Fourth, the purchaser should obtain from the vendor a written direction to the tenant informing the tenant of the change of ownership and directing that future rental payments should be made payable to the new owner.

10. Fire insurance

In some real estate transactions, the fire insurance policy of the vendor is transferred or assigned to the purchaser at the time of closing. Such transfer or assignment requires the consent of the insurance company. If the transfer or assignment is delivered on the closing of the transaction and at that time forwarded to the insurance company or the insurance agent to obtain consent, there could be a lapse of insurance coverage on the house.

This would come about since, at the time of closing, the insurance company had not approved the purchaser and, therefore, the purchaser would not be covered and neither would the vendor because, from the closing date onward, the vendor is no longer the owner of the property and thus would not have an insurable interest.

To avoid this possibility, the insurance company should be advised of the details prior to closing and an agreement should be obtained to protect the interest of the purchaser after closing until such time as the insurance company receives the transfer or assignment document.

11. Hotels, motels, and apartment houses

As a hotel, motel, auto court, apartment house, or rooming house, among others, is considered to be a business, section 29 of the Real Estate Act applies to the sale.

This section provides that whenever a business is being sold the agent shall, before a binding interim agreement is signed, deliver to the purchaser a profit and loss statement showing revenues and expenses of the business for a period of 12 months ending not more than 120 days before the signing of the interim agreement, together with a statement of assets and liabilities of the business and a statement containing a list of fixtures and chattels. It is also a requirement that every such statement be signed by the vendor or the vendor's agent.

e. SERVICES THE VENDOR'S LAWYER WILL PROVIDE

As mentioned previously, normally the vendor's lawyer plays a minor role in the purchase and sale of real estate. Nevertheless, it is an important role as the same lawyer cannot act for both the vendor and the purchaser in a transaction.

The vendor's lawyer will normally check and review any conveyancing documents prepared by the purchaser's lawyer, arrange the signing of the conveyancing documents by the vendor, and enter into undertakings with the purchaser's lawyer with respect to paying the purchase price and/or discharging old mortgages.

When a mortgage is taken back by the vendor, the lawyer will check the mortgage for the vendor and make sure that the mortgage is registered properly so that the vendor has good title to the mortgage. The lawyer will also make sure that the vendor obtains fire insurance protection for the insurable interest.

When the transaction has been completed, the vendor's lawyer will then send a report to the vendor advising that the transaction has closed, giving the registration particulars, and accounting to the vendor for the purchase funds. The vendor's lawyer should also make sure that the real estate commission has, in fact, been paid to the real estate agent either by him- or herself or by the purchaser's lawyer.

Quite often a lawyer acts as the vendor's lawyer on the sale of a client's old home and as the purchaser's lawyer on the purchase of that client's new home.

If the two transactions close almost concurrently, the lawyer can have a "direction" signed by the clients which directs that the sales proceeds of the old home be forwarded directly to the lawyer, thus avoiding the necessity of depositing the funds from the sale of the old home into a bank account and subsequently drawing a certified cheque for the amount of money required for the purchase of the new home.

10

FORECLOSURE AND OTHER REMEDIES FOR DEFAULT UNDER A MORTGAGE

If a person owes money under either a mortgage or an agreement for sale and neglects to make the payments as required under that mortgage or agreement for sale, a number of alternative courses of action are available to the person to whom the money is owed. That person can foreclose on the property, or sue for the arrears owing, or, by exercising the power of sale given in the mortgage, enter onto the property, or exercise the statutory right of sale.

a. FORECLOSURE

Foreclosure is the most common remedy used by the lender in British Columbia today. The primary aim of a foreclosure proceeding is to liquidate the security that was given for the mortgage loan. This is done by taking court action to obtain title to the property — unless there are other encumbrances with higher priority to the charge that is being foreclosed on.

For example, a successful foreclosure by a second lender removes the interest of the third lender and any persons holding judgments against the registered owner and registered after the second mortgage. The second lender becomes a registered owner subject only to the first mortgage.

Foreclosure action is begun by issuing a petition in the Supreme Court of British Columbia with the lender as petitioner and all the people who have an interest in the property ranking behind the lender as respondents.

The respondents include any subsequent mortgage holders and any people with judgments registered against the property owner. The remedies asked for in the petition include an accounting of all money owing, under the mortgage, foreclosure of all the respondents' interest in the property, personal judgment for the amount owing against all the parties personally liable on the debt (the people taking out the mortgage and any guarantors), the appointment of a receiver, possession of the property, *lis pendens,* and cost of the action.

When the petition is issued, a lis pendens (i.e., pending action notice) is obtained from the court registrar and is registered immediately in the Land Title Office to prevent any dealings with the property until the foreclosure action has been completed or abandoned.

After the petition and affidavits in support, which set out the particulars of the default under the mortgage and the particulars of the mortgage, have been served on all the respondents, the petitioner (the lender) can apply in Supreme Court chambers for an order *nisi.*

The order nisi directs an accounting to be taken before the registrar of all money owing under the mortgage and prescribes the manner of providing the amount owing under the mortgage. The order nisi also directs that the respondents, or any one of them, may redeem the mortgage by paying into court the amount found to be owing by the registrar within the specified time.

The specified time is usually six months from the date the registrar takes the accounting, but this period may be reduced or extended depending on the circumstances. Usually, if the property being foreclosed is revenue-producing property (such as a boarding house) or if the foreclosure is of an agreement for sale, the redemption period will be three months.

If the property being foreclosed is residential property being lived in by the respondents, the redemption period will usually be six months (three months under an agreement for sale) unless such time period could cause the petitioner further damages. At the end of the six months, if there is a likelihood that the borrower will be in a position to redeem the mortgage, it is quite often possible that the redemption period could be further extended.

In addition, if the property is rented, the court may appoint a receiver to collect the rents and generally to manage and administer the property. Such a receiver is an officer of the court and the remuneration of that receiver is added to the amount payable to redeem the mortgage. The appointment of a receiver, of course, will be made only if requested by the lender.

If payment has not been made within the redemption period or any extension period granted, the lender then goes back to court and applies for an order absolute. The issuance of the order absolute bars the interest of all the respondents in the property, orders them to deliver possession of the property, and gives judgment for the amount owing, plus costs, against the people personally liable on the debt. The lender, after obtaining the order absolute, can do one of two things.

First, the lender can apply in the Land Title Office for a certificate of title and, after it has been issued, can deal with the property as his or her own. If the property is sold at a profit, the lender can keep the profit. Once this is done, registration of the new certificate of title automatically releases all people liable to pay the mortgage from their liability. In other words, the personal judgment can no longer be enforced.

The lender can also apply under the Land Title Act for an interim certificate of title and can proceed to execute on the judgment for the amount owing against the respondents. If the lender collects anything at all, the foreclosure order may be reopened, since a lower amount would then be necessary to redeem the mortgage.

If the property is being foreclosed by a first lender and there is a second lender, the second lender may, for protection, decide to bring the first mortgage into good standing by paying that mortgage up to date plus costs, then adding such amounts on to his or her mortgage, and commencing foreclosure proceedings.

The registered owner or the second lender can also ask for a sale of the property to protect his or her rights. Such an order for sale given by the court prevents the first lender from proceeding, as discussed above, to sell the property at a profit and keep the profit.

Usually what happens is that the property is sold and the first lender is paid off, including costs, and the proceeds over and above that amount are paid to the next charge holder, and so on down the line.

A person in the position of being foreclosed who cannot, at the time in question, afford to redeem the mortgage or agreement for sale should file an "appearance" at the courthouse and mail or personally deliver to the lawyer handling the foreclosure a copy of the appearance in order to be served with copies of all the court proceedings.

An "appearance" is a simple form that can be obtained from any legal stationer and completed without the help of a lawyer. It does not cost anything to file an appearance. However, if there is any equity in the house, professional help should be sought to protect that equity. This should be done even though there may not be ready cash available to pay for such help; most lawyers would be prepared to offer assistance in such circumstances provided the situation is properly explained to them initially.

b. THE CONTRACTUAL RIGHT OF SALE

In British Columbia, the contractual right of sale — that is, the right of sale given by the mortgage itself — does, in fact, exist. This is not a major remedy used in British Columbia since the registrar of titles will not, under our Land Title Act, register such an instrument.

There is argument that a transfer of the property, signed by the lender exercising the contractual right of sale, is not in accordance with the provisions of the Land Title Act. Although there is also some legal opinion in the province of British Columbia to the contrary, it is a method that is full of problems and should not be undertaken without professional help.

c. THE JUDICIAL SALE OR PRIVATE SALE

A lender or owner can also apply for a judicial sale or private sale. A judicial sale is usually made by public auction with leave of the court. The terms and conditions of sale are fixed by the court both for a private sale and a judicial sale.

A private sale is the usual procedure. The property is valued by two qualified appraisers and listed with a real estate firm. This procedure costs less and is less cumbersome than a public auction.

If the proceeds from the sale are less than the mortgage debt and costs, the lender may proceed to sue on the personal promise to pay to recover any deficiency. The proceeds of the sale are paid into court and all charges are paid off in accordance with their respective priority. If there is any balance left after the charges are paid, it will go to the owner.

The judicial sale, of course, is not a worthwhile remedy for a lender to ask for since it is of no advantage to the lender whatsoever. It is usually the borrower or a subsequent charge holder who asks for a judicial sale.

d. THE MORTGAGOR AS TENANT

Most mortgages, until the passing of the amendments to the Residential Tenancy Act, provided that the borrower become a "tenant" of the lender. In effect, it created a relationship of landlord and tenant between the borrower and the lender.

221

The effect of this clause was that the lender had the right to seize the borrower's goods for arrears of mortgage payments. It granted the lender a right to enter the premises peaceably once default had been made, seize the goods of the borrower, and use them or sell them to compensate for the default.

More detail on this is not really required since the distress aspect of the mortgage is very seldom used in British Columbia. This is true especially in view of the amendments to the Residential Tenancy Act which makes distress illegal in residential properties unless the property has been abandoned. As a result of this amendment and the fact that its implications with respect to mortgages are not entirely clear, some lawyers drawing mortgages on behalf of the lender delete this clause altogether.

11

YOUR HOME AND TAXES

One of the great benefits of home ownership is that the primary residence of a home owner is not subject to capital gains tax. Thus, if our friends Harry and Hilda Homeseeker, who bought their home for $89 000, turn around two years later and sell it for $139 000, the $50 000 increase is tax free.

However, only the house and up to one acre surrounding the house are automatically tax free. When the house is situated on more than one acre, the general test applied by the tax department is, "Can the property over one acre reasonably be regarded as necessary for the use and enjoyment of the residents?" Such factors as the landscaping plan, location of the home on the property, and subdivision regulations of the local municipality are all considered.

a. ARE YOU OPERATING A RENOVATIONS BUSINESS?

Jack Carpenter had discovered that he could buy an older run-down house, fix it up while living in it with his family, and then sell it and move on to the next old home that needed repairs. He had done so approximately six times in the last two years.

Suddenly, one day he received a reassessment from the tax department. They had taken all of the profits that he had made on all the houses that he had renovated since starting this method of operation and added it all back into his income, disagreeing with his allocation of profits as capital gains. They then taxed him on these new figures.

223

By the frequency of his transactions, Jack had established that his intent was not just to live there but also to make money by fixing up the homes and selling them. The tax department had taken the position that what he was doing was a business and had taxed him accordingly.

What is the difference between this and the case where you fix your house and later find it is not to your liking? A sale here is not in the course of business and would be tax free. Probably the main factor is the number of times you buy and sell over a certain period. Once is okay, probably twice — but beyond that it gets tricky.

Also note that an additionally owned piece of property, such as a recreational property, can be depreciated and expenses written off if you declare the property "commercial" by placing it on the rental market. Most people do not use such property frequently and the tax write-offs gained may be well worth the inconvenience of having it available for rental purposes. Talk it over with your accountant and get some figures on paper. Of course, if this is done, you lose the capital gain tax-free status but this is minimized with the income tax exemption and the tax savings gained by converting the premises to commercial use can be substantial. This is especially so if you are paying interest on a mortgage (the major cost of any dwelling) which can then be written off (less that portion pertaining to your personal use).

As mentioned previously under the section dealing with vendor financing, some vendors are prepared to leave some of the equity in their primary residence when they sell it, provided the equity is secured by a mortgage. Any interest earned from such a mortgage is income.

If a vendor finds that it is easier to sell a home by asking perhaps slightly more for the home but offering a lower interest rate on the financing, the vendor will be much better off even though the total amount paid by the vendor is the same. This is because the higher purchase price is tax free while the higher interest earned is fully taxable.

Likewise, in situations where the vendors of the house are joint owners but in different income tax brackets, the sale should be structured in such a way that the person with the higher income tax bracket is fully paid out while the person with the lower income tax bracket provides the financing so that all interest income is taxed at the lower rate.

b. WHAT ABOUT RENTING YOUR HOME?

If you and your family are planning to travel or perhaps be away on an extended business trip you may be considering the possibility of renting your home. You must be careful about the tax implications in this case because the Income Tax Act says that, as soon as you rent your home, you are deemed to have disposed of it and, when you return, to have reacquired it at fair market value. With the rapid rise in property value during these inflationary times, this will subject you to both a taxable capital gain as commercial property and a recapture of the capital cost allowance which you would be charging as an expense to offset the rental income.

Faced with this, you are probably better off making an election under section 45(2) of the Income Tax Act, which allows you to maintain your home as "principal residence" and thus keep it free of capital gains tax for up to four years even though you may not ordinarily "inhabit" the house.

During this time you may not claim capital cost allowance and the rental income must be subject to tax. You are still allowed to charge against income the normal operating expenses such as heat, light, insurance, maintenance, mortgage interest, and taxes.

As long as you have not claimed any capital cost allowance you would normally be allowed to make this election after the rental period has started.

c. ARE YOU RENTING PART OF YOUR HOME OR OPERATING A BUSINESS OUT OF IT?

You may be interested in renting out part of your home or, perhaps, operating a business out of the basement. In this case you must again be careful about the "principal" residence status of your home. Where part of the principal residence is set aside for the purpose of earning income, then a reasonable proportion of the expenses such as utilities, insurance, mortgage interest, and taxes can be deducted as expenses against your income. You should be careful again, however, not to charge capital cost allowance, as this will change your property from residential to commercial and the house will lose its capital gains tax-free status. For more information, contact your accountant or your nearest district tax office.

d. MAKING YOUR MORTGAGE INTEREST TAX DEDUCTIBLE

Under normal circumstances, interest paid on a mortgage on the home is not deductible expense for income tax purposes. However, interest expense incurred for the purpose of earning income is deductible.

So, if a mortgage is taken out on the home, and all or part of the proceeds are used for investing, the interest on the mortgage applicable to such portion used for investing is deductible even if no income was in fact earned. Therefore, if you receive a large sum of money, it would be advantageous, rather than investing it directly, to pay off the mortgage, then refinance and invest. The interest on the mortgage would then be deductible.

e. OTHER TAX CONSIDERATIONS WITH RECENT CHANGES

For the taxation years from 1994 on, there will no longer be a capital gains exemption. A husband and wife together can have only one primary residence.

Interest-free or low-interest housing loans provided to employees through their employer (such as a bank or financial institution) are exempt from tax. However, this exemption applies only where the person has begun employment at a new location in Canada after May 23, 1985, and where the employee's new residence is at least 40 km closer to the new job location than the previous residence. The maximum annual tax-free benefit is equivalent to the taxable benefit from an interest-free housing loan of $25 000, and is available for a maximum period of five years.

12

MISCELLANEOUS MATTERS

a. HOME IMPROVEMENTS

Once in the home, you may wish to renovate, remodel, or make an addition. Whether this takes the form of tearing out a wall, adding an extra room, or building a carport or swimming pool, there are various legal and business matters that must be considered and dealt with prior to beginning the work.

First, you should make sure that the zoning bylaw will allow you to make the proposed alteration or addition. There would be a problem, for example, when the addition or renovation would change the use of the property from a single family dwelling to a multiple family dwelling or from a residential dwelling into a partly residential and partly commercial building.

Second, the zoning bylaw usually contains setback requirements. These setback requirements are minimum distances from the various lot lines on which a home owner is prohibited from erecting any permanent construction. In other words, if the setback requirements are a minimum of one metre from the side borders of the property, the carport cannot be built closer than one metre to the side property lines.

However, if the proposed addition or alteration is in contravention of the zoning bylaw to a minor extent, it is possible to make an application to the Board of Variance in the municipality in which the property is located to get consent to the minor variance. Once the Board of Variance approves the variance, you can proceed with the alterations.

Also, when considering an addition, you should make sure it is not built on an easement or right-of-way on the property. The owner of the easement or right-of-way could later force you to remove the addition.

Before any renovations, additions, or alterations can take place, you must first obtain a building permit from the building department of the municipality. Depending on the size of the alteration or addition, the building department may require detailed plans of the proposed alteration. The fee charged on the building permit is, in most instances, based upon the value attributable to the alterations or additions.

The purpose of the building permit is essentially three-fold. First, it enables the municipality to check that all alterations are done according to the standards required by the municipality. If you are doing the work this is probably a disadvantage because, unless you are experienced at such things, there will inevitably be mistakes which you will have to correct at extra cost to yourself. On the other hand, you may welcome someone who is able to carefully review your work. If you hire a contractor, you should, for your own protection, make sure a permit is taken out. The cost of a permit is quite low and the building inspector acts as your safeguard in ensuring the work is up to standard.

Second, it raises revenue for the municipality. Third, it provides the municipality with information about the value of the additions to the property so that it can be taken into account when the next assessment is done for property tax purposes.

For more extensive renovations and for renovations where a contractor is involved, reference should also be made to the new home sections in chapter 3, including the one on builders' liens.

b. SUBDIVIDING

Subdividing, itself, could be the subject of a book and is, therefore, dealt with only briefly.

Before a piece of property can be subdivided, it must not, of course, be subject to the provincial government's land freeze. It must also comply with the zoning bylaws governing the particular area in which it is situated. Whether or not the property will meet these prerequisites can be determined by consulting with the planning department of the municipality in which the property is located.

If the property is located in unorganized territory, the highways department in whose jurisdiction the property is located must be consulted.

Before the appropriate approving authority will give its permission for the subdivision, it will, in most instances, require the person subdividing to pay certain fees to the municipality and/or install certain services such as roads, sewers, electricity, water, power, and drainage.

Although there are rules and regulations governing the fees that can be charged, many municipalities will attempt to extract as much money as they possibly can from the person who wishes to subdivide. This is a specialized area, and, therefore, if you feel that you are being unfairly treated by the municipal authorities, seek professional help to challenge them.

Unless it is a very simple subdivision such as dividing lot X evenly into two, thus creating, for example, the south half and the north half of lot X, a surveyor will be required to draw a subdivision plan. This subdivision plan must be signed by the surveyor, the approving officer for the municipality (or highways department in unorganized territory), the owner, and all encumbrance holders before it is submitted to the Land Title Office for registration.

Once filed for registration, the subdivision plan is given a number and a new legal description is created for the subdivided properties. If five or more lots are created by the subdivision, a vendor is required to file a real estate prospectus with the Superintendent of Insurance before being allowed to sell the lots to anyone (see also the section dealing with the real estate prospectus in chapter 3). Subdividing is a complex area and, unless a person is knowledgeable in the area, professional help should be sought.

c. INVESTING IN MORTGAGES

Investing in mortgages is a popular investment for many people. The rate of return can vary from market interest rates for first mortgages to twice that rate or even more for second or third mortgages. There is usually a direct correlation between the rate of return and the risk factor that can be summarized by saying that the higher the return, the higher the risk.

Most investing is done through mortgage brokers who find the borrower, write the mortgage, and then sell it. When dealing with a mortgage broker, whether you are arranging a loan or investing, you should be as selective and careful as when dealing with a used car salesperson.

Generally speaking, the mortgage broker, or the person selling the mortgage, will be responsible for preparing all legal documentation to assign the mortgage to the investor and will bear the costs of doing so.

When investing in a mortgage, you should check or verify the following basic essentials before the purchase money is paid over:

(a) The legal description in the mortgage and the civic address of the property which is mortgaged should correspond and should represent the same property.

(b) There should be insurance on the property for an amount equal, at least, to the outstanding amounts of all the mortgages with loss payable to the assignee of the mortgage as his or her interest may appear.

(c) The balance owing on the mortgage and the monthly payments should be confirmed by the person making the payments.

(d) Not only should the mortgage be assigned and the assignment registered in the Land Title Office, but a notice of the assignment should also be completed and given to the person making the payments.

(e) The investor should be satisfied that there is some equity in the property. The more equity there is, the more protection. The less equity there is, the higher the interest rate. The investor must decide whether it is better to receive a higher interest rate and bear a higher risk or receive a lower interest rate and bear a lower risk. If there is no equity in the property, there is very little incentive to the mortgagor to make the payments.

(f) The investment money should be paid not to the mortgage broker but only to the broker's lawyer against a written undertaking not to release the money until the required mortgage interest is obtained. Money can also be paid to the investor's own lawyer, who will then look after and protect the investor's interests. The investor will, unless it has been negotiated otherwise, be responsible for that lawyer's fees. A short time after registration, the investor should also receive a state of title certificate from the lawyer handling the transaction indicating the registration particulars and the nature and priority of the charge.

(g) As mentioned, generally speaking it is the mortgage broker who pays for the cost of assigning the mortgage to the investor. In any event, the investor should clearly ascertain, before purchasing or agreeing to purchase a mortgage, who will be paying the lawyer.

(h) An investor should also be aware of an obscure provincial statute before investing in farm lands. The name of the statute is the Agricultural Land Development Act. Section 9 of this act provides that a loan made under this act by the government may, when in default, be added to the property taxes and would thus, in essence, take priority over all other charges. Loans under this act are made for clearing and developing land. In other words, what the investor thought was a first mortgage may later become a second!

(i) Mortgage brokerage is governed by the Mortgage Brokers Act. This act provides that, where the borrower is charged with a brokerage fee or a commission, the borrower is required to be presented with a disclosure statement before signing the mortgage. This disclosure statement gives full disclosure to the borrower of the true cost of the mortgage. The borrower should be supplied with three copies of the disclosure statement. The borrower may file such a statement with the Land Title Office within 48 hours of signing it and request that the mortgage be rescinded. The borrower, upon return of all the money advanced under the mortgage, is entitled to rescind the mortgage at any time. Therefore, an investor should also obtain a copy of the disclosure statement from the mortgage broker.

For further information about mortgages in general, please refer to chapters 5 and 6.

If you have enjoyed this book and would like to receive a free catalogue of all Self-Counsel titles, please write to:

Self-Counsel Press
1481 Charlotte Road
North Vancouver, B.C.
V7J 1H1